WOMAN
ON A SEESAW

WOMAN ON A SEESAW

The Ups and Downs of Making It

Hilary Cosell

G. P. PUTNAM'S SONS
New York

G. P. Putnam's Sons
Publishers Since 1838
200 Madison Avenue
New York, NY 10016

The author gratefully acknowledges permission from the
following sources to reprint material in their control:
Harcourt Brace Jovanovich, Inc., The Hogarth Press Ltd.,
and the Author's Literary Estate for an excerpt from
A Room of One's Own by Virginia Woolf,
copyright 1929 by Harcourt Brace Jovanovich, Inc.;
renewed 1957 by Leonard Woolf.
The New York Times for material from
"Why Radcliffe Women Are Afraid of Success"
by Vivian Gornick in the magazine of January 14, 1973,
copyright © 1973 by The New York Times Company.

Library of Congress Cataloging in Publication Data

Cosell, Hilary, date.
Woman on a seesaw.

1. Women in the professions—United States.
2. Success. 3. Married women—Employment—United States.
4. Happiness. 5. Choice (Psychology) I. Title.
HQ1426.C73 1985   305.4'3'0973   84-18043
ISBN 0-399-13034-9

Printed in the United States of America
1 2 3 4 5 6 7 8 9 10

This book is dedicated to three very special women:
my friend Nancy Whitcomb;
my sister Jill;
and my mother Emmy.
. . . and to the Coach.

Contents

When a subject is highly controversial—and any question about sex is that—one cannot hope to tell the truth. One can only show how one came to hold the opinion one does hold. One can only give one's audience the chance of drawing their own conclusions as they observe the limitations, the prejudices, the idiosyncrasies of the speaker. . . . Lies will flow from my lips, but there may perhaps be some truth mixed up with them; it is for you to seek out this truth and to decide whether any part of it is worth keeping.

Virginia Woolf, *A Room of One's Own*

Introduction

L ately I've been thinking a lot about someone named Gregor Samsa.

He's the one who went to sleep one night a perfectly normal person and woke up the next morning transformed into a giant insect. This happens in a story called "The Metamorphosis," by Franz Kafka, and to be honest, I've never been much of a Kafka fan. But I always rather liked Gregor and sometimes I wish he were real. I think we have something in common and perhaps we could chat.

Of course my metamorphosis, if I can call it that, didn't occur overnight, and I didn't turn into a bug either. No, whatever happened to me took several years at least, and most of the time I wasn't even aware of the changes.

This is who I was: a liberal, a humanist, a registered

Democrat. A dove, a leftist, a civil rights activist, an antinuclear anything at all. A New Yorker and a journalist. Well fed, well educated, and reasonably well shod. White, solidly middle class, and probably a typical product of my time, place, and socioeconomic group. A successful network television sports producer, sometime on-camera correspondent, and a vocal feminist.

I am still many of those things.

This is who I am now: a person confused, skeptical, wary, unsure. Not about war versus peace, or left versus right, but about women. About the wealth of choices women are said to enjoy only twenty years after the publication of *The Feminine Mystique.* About the wisdom of believing that solutions to fundamental conflicts between traditional female roles and today's newer ones can be so easily found, or easily implemented. About women and success. Sometimes I think nothing could be more naive and misguided than the simplistic belief that access to title and income and the corporation—success—could wipe away the inequalities of the past, or change the way men perceive women, or women perceive themselves.

This is what you might label me: conservative or reactionary. Someone who couldn't take the heat and got out of the kitchen. A retreater into traditional "gutless" femininity. Perhaps even antifeminist.

I am none of those things.

This is what happened: for five years I traveled almost every week. I interviewed athletes and coaches, team owners and player reps. I attended spring training and football camp. Went to the King Dome, the Silver

Dome, the Super Dome. The Orange Bowl, the Rose Bowl, and the Super Bowl. I covered thoroughbred racing and auto racing. I ran the gamut and ran the gauntlet too.

It sounds glamorous, and some of it was. It sounds like fun, and much of it was. It sounds "interesting" and "rewarding," and most of it was. It sounds like hard work, and all of it was.

But the hardest part wasn't getting interviews or finding stories or even getting air time. The hardest part was pretending. Pretending can be just exhausting.

I got tired of pretending to be "politically sound" and "ideologically pure." I'm not talking about pretending to vote Republican when I pulled the Democratic lever, or espousing conservative doctrine while counting the days till a liberal moved back into the White House.

I mean that I got tired of being correct from what you might call a hard-core feminist viewpoint.

First, take something simple enough, such as "dressing for success." All the how-tos, the manuals, the do's and don'ts. Mostly don'ts. Don't look too masculine but be especially careful not to look too feminine. No ribbons, no bows, no ruffles, no lace, no dresses, watch the hemline, watch the neckline, no straight skirts, chuck the perfume, pearls only, a light hand with the makeup, pastels preferred, please. Don't be yourself. Be professional. On guard, and don't draw attention to your sex.

Then couple that with the primer on aggression and assertiveness. Be the latter, not the former. Aggression is masculine, a turn-off, but assertiveness is professional, correct, the right way. Quite frankly, I could never really

14

tell the difference between the two, and—let's face it—aggression is what gets results and rewards. But after all the talk about women learning to be aggressive and unafraid to show it, there we were, trying to put the lid on it and walk some tightrope between assertive and aggressive.

Next, add the robot game: remaining calm, emotionless, bloodless really, all the time, while the men around you feel free to fling fits and objects at the slightest provocation. But no matter how much right you may have to blow your stack, chew people out, don't do it. They'll call you a castrater, a bitch. Or, worst of all, they'll shake their heads and say, "See, we knew women couldn't take the pressure. Crazy. Unstable. All hormones."

All this was tiresome enough—this worry about clothing and aggression and acting like a computer instead of a person—and none of it, you notice, has anything at all to do with the work a woman is doing or how well she does it. But it was the pretense about success that was the real killer. The constant pressure to prove that one is every bit as success-oriented as the boy in the next office is said to be.

I was success-oriented and I am success-oriented. I remain ambitious, competitive, and in need of work for my own self-esteem. But at the same time, I can no longer pretend that success itself is my *modus vivendi.* And though it was once my *modus operandi,* too, it is less important to me now. Especially given the fact that my definition of success doesn't have much to do with corporate America's, or with what now appears to be the feminist definition of success as well.

15

Success in their terms doesn't have much to do with the quality of one's work, or a commitment to excellence in terms of one's ability or one's product. Generally it doesn't seem to matter much how one performs on a job, as long as it's merely average, marginally competent, and essentially conformist and pedestrian.

Success by their definition means: What's your title, how much do you earn, and how much power do you wield? And the ability to obtain those three things depends largely on one thing: How much of a team player are you? And that means: To what lengths will a person go to prove to an employer that the organization always comes first? How often will you sacrifice family and friends, lovers, spouses, and children, as well as yourself, for the sake of the corporation? If a person is unwilling to do this, not *some* of the time, but whenever, however, and how often it is asked of them, then success is probably out of the question. Instead, you'll raise uncomfortable questions about loyalties and priorities; appear unserious and uncommitted. Perhaps even reduce the level of productivity, the original sin in the bible of business.

In order to become successful, a certain amount of sacrifice of a personal life is an absolute necessity. That sacrifice can be painful, draining, and even boring.

This sacrifice is often extremely difficult for many men. How much more difficult is it for women, who face questions of biology and childbirth? Who face choices that men do not really have to face at all?

Right now, the conventional wisdom says women can "have it all." No longer must they choose between

16

career and children, the marketplace and the kitchen. The potential conflict between the two is ignored or glossed over, dismissed with jolly little self-help articles about selecting the day care that's right for you, or tips on how to say goodbye to your hysterical three-year-old who doesn't want you to leave that morning.

It's more complicated than that. Worse, we leave these questions mostly unexamined. We pretend. Having it all sounds so wonderful, so upwardly mobile, so right, so American. It's so popular it has to be possible. The new American female birthright.

What's happened is that women have fallen hook, line, and sinker for a terribly narrow, restrictive male definition of what it means to succeed. For more than fifteen years we have blindly accepted income, title, and power as our gods, exchanged them for home, hearth, and children. We have fought to mold ourselves into reasonable facsimiles of the men whose status in the professional world was a source of envy. And we did it by insisting that women, given the opportunity and the chance to compete, were basically no different from the men who excluded them by law, custom, and tradition.

Now, slowly, reluctantly, a whole generation of women are facing issues and choices that a previous generation of women spent little time discussing. Is it possible to have it all and do it all? Are there some very different demands for women, needs that must be fulfilled, in order for a woman to feel successful? Needs outside of an office? Do we face not a cornucopia of choices, but a nightmare of options, none of them very good?

This is a book about some women of this generation, and for others like them. Women who fashioned themselves upon the male model of success only to find themselves questioning all or part of almost everything they once believed to be true. About themselves and success. About choices they made in favor of a career at the possible expense of their personal lives. About women who are coming to grips with the knowledge that differences between men and women—whether biological or sociological in origin, or both—cannot just be ignored. Women who are learning the hard way that a wide gulf separates "being your own person" and financial independence from being "successful." And especially about women who are looking for ways and means to modify the definition of success and redefine it in more flexible terms for women.

This is not a self-help book, nor a survival guide, nor a how-to manual. Nor is it a sociological survey of two thousand women and their attitudes toward success today.

It is not my intention to portray my choices, compromises, and decisions as the right ones, the final ones, or even the best ones. Nor is it my intention to send women back to the kitchen and nursery, or decry as frauds those who have found happiness or contentedness in their ability to successfully combine several identities into a workable whole, or criticize those who had little or no trouble making choices.

Rather, it is my aim to describe, not proscribe. Through interviews with a variety of successful professional women between the ages of twenty-six and forty, from all parts of the country, this book attempts to increase the awareness of women and men alike regarding the conflicts and hard choices women face concerning career, success, and themselves as females.

The disparity between what women say publicly about these issues and what they say privately to other women is immense. Because of it, very few of the women I spoke to would agree to be interviewed without a guarantee of anonymity. Not one appears here without an alias. And nearly all of them feared professional, not personal, reprisal. Nearly all confided things they believed would injure their images as professionals, the postures they maintain at work, the pretending.

Hilary Cosell
New York City, 1984

1

Ms.givings

I think we all grew up knowing something about everything except limitation. If our generation has a curse upon it, like generations are sometimes said to have, ours is believing we can have it all. Somehow those of us who grew up in the sixties, in that spirit of freedom and choice and rebellion and commitment to change, came of age and transformed into adults who are as materialistic, conformist and greedy as we thought our parents were and despised them for being. Perhaps even worse. And when I look around me, the strongest indication of it is what has happened to women and the women's movement. Money, power, title, corporation, business, success. It bewilders me. We didn't start out that way. We wanted to open things up. Instead, we constricted them. What happened? Ten years ago I had all the answers. Today, I have nothing but questions.

I never forgot the commercial.

A montage of fashionable women flashed by in cityscape after cityscape. Woman after woman, each looking more attractive, more important, more in control than her predecessor. Smart tailored suits, attaché cases, shapely pumps, heels clicking on the pavement, legs striding down streets, up stairs, into skyscrapers to rest behind big desks. Makeup perfect, every hair in place in sleek chignons or other graceful, classic hair styles. All projecting an image that said: confident, purposeful, serious. I am a woman who matters. I make a difference.

I think the ad was for a bank and it ran in the early sixties. Needless to say, it made a lasting impression on me. Somehow it fitted right in with the message my collection of Nancy Drews and biographies of Susan B. Anthony, Amelia Earhart, Margaret Bourke-White, and

Babe Zaharias sent me. Do something. Be somebody. Grow up to be a woman who counts.

Memory plays tricks, of course, but I think it was the first ad I ever saw in which women weren't portrayed as housewives shilling for cleanser, mothers waxing rhapsodic over detergents or, as little sex kittens, offering themselves as a bonus if you bought their product. Though the women in my ad were obviously models, and there was heavy emphasis on their looks, there was still something different about it. They were businesswomen. Professionals. Successful.

The implications were clear, impressive, and outside the norm of my upper middle class Westchester County world, where mommies didn't work because no mommies "had" to work. So I kept the memory of that ad stored someplace inside me, buried it for future use. A secret, silent motivator. Through my flower-child Fillmore East days, my antiwar years, my style that consisted of two pairs of jeans, a few T-shirts, waist-length hair and no makeup, I never forgot. One day I'll shed this skin and become that. Caterpillar into a butterfly—and I wasn't referring to my looks.

I found a partner to guide me through the tug-of-war taking place inside me during high school, something to remind me that popularity and partying were great, but so was early acceptance by an Ivy League school. I found the women's movement. It reinforced and amplified everything I thought myself, and more.

The days of finding personal reward in being the woman behind the successful man were over. Finished. The days of defining one's worth by the presence of a man, or lack of worth by the absence of one, were over. A woman's place was anywhere she chose to make that place, and if men refused to graciously concede the rightness of our position, we'd take to the streets and the courts to make sure the days of discrimination and second-class citizenry were finished too. In the hearts and minds, as well as the laws, of men. And women.

We had to do it right, though. All the way down the line. Adhere to a position in every part of life. We wouldn't succeed by displaying any traditional kinds of female behavior. No, those had to go, too. What was femininity, anyway, but a male creation? First they shackled our bodies with their silly, restrictive definitions of what was fashion, and what was beauty, and what was the proper height, weight, leg length, breast size, hair color, and eye color. Then they shackled our minds, taught us that ambition, aggression, brains, talent, drive, ruthlessness, independence were all their birthrights. Women who displayed these traits were unfeminine, unattractive, unworthy. The proper province for whatever aggression and drive and competition women had was to compete for male attention and male approval. To win a man and then keep him. By softness, passivity, dependence, nurturing, peacemaking. Control and power by indirect manipulation, all designed to feed the male ego, the male sense of his due, the male definition of his world and everyone else's place in it.

The movement laid it all out for me to see, and when they finished, womankind looked like some washed-up old whore all decked out for one final trick on her bier before retiring to meet her maker. Male, of course. I was

24

aghast. Outraged. So full of righteous anger and indignation I didn't know which way was up or down. Or whom I was more angry with—men for thousands of years of mistreating women, or women for allowing themselves to be willing partners in their own destruction.

And nothing condensed the horror of it all better than the thought that I could wind up condemned to a lifetime of servitude in a kitchen and a nursery. Marriage was a prison, and suburbia death, and children a lifetime of slavery. To end up the dependent and drudge of some man who, if statistics can be trusted, would leave me and our kids six or ten or even twenty years after the ceremony to struggle along on insufficient alimony and child-support payments, most likely in suburbia, was a fate too terrible to contemplate.

No sir, not me. I got the message and the truth set me free. I will be successful. Earn lots of money, be a professional. Ah! I uttered the word in tones usually reserved for brief mentions of the Father, Son, and Holy Ghost. Or a major financial coup. Not a career girl, someone filing her nails at her desk, earning a pittance and marking time between college and a husband. Not a working woman, either, doing unskilled, unglamorous work in the pink-collar ghetto.

No, I got the message right, figured out what was being said amid the shouting, finger-pointing, and epithet-hurling. Women are entitled to success. To a real piece of the action. To the American dream. Upscale and upmarket. Upwardly mobile. Today a Jones, tomorrow a Rockefeller, and everyone will be trying to keep up with you. To the job and the money that will buy a house and two cars, a condo and a boat, the TV, the VCR, the Atari, stocks and bonds, tax shelters, whatever is your pleasure and whatever makes you happy.

It sounds pretty good. It makes sense. Why shouldn't women have a chance at these things? Why should they belong almost exclusively to the white male establishment? Besides, if one becomes successful, one is supposed to reap all sorts of extra rewards besides material goods. Happiness and fulfillment. Respect and recognition. Sometimes even fame. Success will make you more popular, more desirable. An object of other people's envy. At the top of everyone's guest list. In demand. And naturally, more desirable than ever before to the opposite sex. Even though one is no longer supposed to care anything at all about whether they find you desirable or not.

And of course success meant other things, too. It meant freedom from economic and emotional dependence on men. It meant you were a special person, a brave and strong pioneer out there fighting the good fight. Hacking your way through the jungle to beat a path for successive generations of women to follow. It made you superior to women without success, several cuts above them. It was proof that you were USDA Prime, while the others were some inferior cut of person. Hiding behind traditional femininity and clutching the very chains that bound them.

But most of all, for anyone of my generation deeply affected by the women's movement, success would make you active, not passive. You would be in control of your fate and your future, the way men are. You would be safe from victimization. You would be *inviolate.* Who could turn it down? How seductive. How alluring.

And so I didn't. After studying history and political science for two years at Sarah Lawrence College—and panicking because it was just too liberal arts, and what was I being *prepared* for?—I transferred to New York University to study journalism. To become prepared to be a reporter. I went one step better and got a master's degree in journalism, so that I could perhaps teach if the newspaper I worked for suddenly folded, as they seem wont to do these days. One day you have a by-line, the next day the unemployment line.

That never happened, though. I couldn't get a newspaper job. So many folded that there were seasoned reporters looking for work, people with ten years' experience covering Congress who were willing to spend their days writing obits, if someone would just hire them. So I went into television. It's an expanding market, you see. Also, it pays much, much better.

I began as a production associate for a network news show. I was a "PA" in TV jargon, the lowest of the low, earning a pittance and too often filing my nails, not marking time between Northwestern and marriage, but trying to figure out how to supplant the four people ahead of me who would get promoted to producer first. Not only did I earn a pittance, but there was no overtime, no sixth- or seventh-day pay. But there was lots of overtime and there were lots of sixth and seventh days. On many of those I spent my time logging every word,

every gesture, pan, zoom, wipe, and cutaway on Geraldo
Rivera videotapes. Or hours on the phone chartering
small planes bound for peculiar destinations. Or setting
up interviews with people whom I would never meet, for
stories I would never help edit, and certainly never come
close to producing. In short the job was insufferable but
the TV business wasn't. And after all, I was in the "paying your dues" phase of the success mythology.

Almost one year later I got my big break. That's part
of the mythology, too. Sooner or later everyone gets the
break and I was just lucky. Mine came sooner and I
jumped. To another network and another show. At
twenty-four I had a new title: network television producer. It seemed to have all paid off: working as a reporter for some Gannett newspapers during college,
exchanging de Tocqueville and democracy for Elementary Reporting and the *AP Handbook,* leaving behind
the serene academic atmosphere of Sarah Lawrence for
the grime and urban blight of NYU. Sure, it was sports,
not news or politics, but nothing's ever perfect.

My life changed almost overnight. Not only did my
income double, triple and climb even more, but I went
from yes-sir-no-sir-anything-you-say-sir to being in
charge. Anything you want to do, you just do it, they
said, smiling. So I traveled back and forth across the
country interviewing athletes, coaches, and team
owners. Boxers, promoters, trainers. Athletes on strike,
athletes contemplating strikes, athletes who refused to
strike. Ones with drug problems, others with alcohol
problems. Born-again athletes, retiring athletes, rookies,
and veterans. I produced a segment called SportsJournal

on a show called "SportsWorld." It was the news part of the show, the journalism, the part that showed we cared about more than who won, or lost, or even how they played the game.

I chose the stories. I researched them. I wrote the scripts. Most of the time I did the interviews. The face people saw, the voice they heard, more often than not never did anything. I picked the music, edited the story, and watched it roll from Studio 6A into millions of homes.

And I understood that I had to look my part. Live my part. Dress for success. The jeans and T-shirts moved to the back of the closet to make way for suits. Designer clothes, all cotton, linen, silk, and wool, as if I wouldn't be real if the fibers weren't too.

So I traveled every week, and talked to famous people, and walked around looking smug, probably. I've got the world on a string. I've done everything differently from my mother's generation. I've done everything right. I have money, and power, and independence, and a profession, and I am inviolate.

So imagine my shock, my near-trauma, when I realized that I wanted something else. Needed something else. When I realized that I loved my job and I hated it. That it was my whole life. That it was no life at all. That somehow, after years of education and what might be called indoctrination into the virtues of success and the worthlessness of female existence without it, I started to feel empty and isolated and desolate. To feel a need for some kind of personal life that was more than casual, or occasional, unstable and rootless.

There I was, coming home from ten or twelve or sometimes more hours at work, pretty much shot after the day, and I'd do this simply marvelous imitation of all the successful fathers I remembered from childhood. All the men I swore I'd never grow up and marry, let alone be like. (Gloria Steinem once said—cheerfully, I believe—we're becoming the men we were supposed to marry. Great.) The men who would come home from the office, grab a drink or two, collapse on the couch, shovel in a meal and be utterly useless for anything beyond the most mundane and desultory conversation. *Boring.* Burned out. And there I'd be, swilling a vodka on the rocks or two, shoving a Stouffer's into my mouth, and then staggering off to take a bath, watch "Hill Street Blues," and fade away with Ted Koppel. To get up and do it all again.

All the time, of course, in the back of my mind, despite protestations otherwise, was the desire to have something more than my profession. To have a personal life, a future, that somehow included a man and possibly children, although motherhood has never been a big priority of mine. Oh, later on, I'd think, I'll work on it later on, next week after I finish this story, next month when spring training concludes, after the owners' meetings, when the football strike ends, sometime I'll get to it. Just let me get on with this career, it's more important, it's the only vital thing in the world.

But somehow, the life I'd managed to construct for myself—coupled with the prevailing attitudes and popular mythology about success and single professional women—seemed to pretty much preclude the possibility of living much differently from the way I already lived. First of all, success demands a full-time commitment. Once you become successful, there's no time to relax, or do less than before. Getting in to become successful is only one-third the battle. Staying there takes up most of one's time and energy, and getting even further ahead takes even more.

And then, our culture pretends that creating a social life as an adult in a large metropolitan area—where there is no sense of community and where the old ties of neighborhood, family, and college days have broken down completely—is something people can just go out and do. If they have a mind to. Join a health club! Work on your favorite candidate's political campaign! Take night classes! Talk about feeling foolish. Talk about wearing a neon sign that proclaims: Lonely, need more friends, looking for love. Talk about . . . desperate. And talk about time. Creating a personal life is a task of immense proportion. Like work, it takes time, and it takes energy. How much is there to go around, especially when life is ordered to make success the priority?

And finally, success demands something more from women than it demands from men. And especially from single women, although the demands on married women and working mothers are equally burdensome in different ways. Successful women are asked to continually prove that the company will get a return on its investment. That they will not run off at the first opportunity to wed. Or to have children. That in exchange for the privilege of an employee ID number and a salary that really should be paid to a guy, women will prove that nothing and no one is more important than the job. That life has few, if any other, considerations. That this is the normal, reasonable price one pays for the honor of being admitted to the club.

If it were only that straightforward perhaps it would have been easier to swallow. Unfortunately, it isn't. Because at the same time, women are also pressured constantly about the status of their personal lives. Don't marry, but why aren't you married? You're twenty-eight? What's wrong with you? Oh, you're married? When are you going to have a baby? Why don't you have a baby? You better not have a baby.

In other words, the messages come thick, fast and constantly—and conflicting—from women and men alike: when are you going to act like a woman? Why don't you act like a woman? Don't act like a woman, there's no place for it here.

One isn't supposed to pay attention to things like that. One is supposed to be free from considerations of what people think. Peer pressure is an adolescent problem, something to put away with other childish things. One simply carries on, pays no attention, does the job, delivers what has been promised, and what's all the fuss about?

Nothing, really, until one realizes that "choosing" success, pursuing it through high school and college and graduate school and on into the business world, is not the simple kind of choice between freedom and bondage people have made it out to be. The battles involved don't cover just things such as comparable pay for comparable work, or a question of learning how to dress, or putting a polite damper on your boss, who's trying to sleep with you.

The price of success is high for everyone, but it is especially high for women, and not just because they fight constant discrimination. For women, the conflicts and the choices involved in dedicating oneself to success are so fundamental, so basic, that sometimes they are unbearable. Conflicts about professional life versus family life, career versus husband and children, and even one's most personal and private perceptions of self and sexual identity.

In order to get ahead, one just dismissed or ignored these conflicts. They were cast aside while we got on with the business of work. Perhaps we refused to acknowledge them in hopes that the problems would just disappear in time. Or because to admit them would give aid and comfort to the enemy: the men and the women who insisted that women belonged in the home and nowhere else. That women couldn't handle a professional life, do the work, take the pressure, compete and succeed. That all women ever want—all that ever makes them happy—is a man and a kid and a home to take care of.

So imagine my surprise when I discovered I could no longer dismiss or ignore my own conflicts and questions. When I started to think that if women had erred once before on the side of marriage and motherhood and housewifery, might they be erring again on the side of professionalism, career, and success? That the extreme to which women have gone for the past fifteen-plus years may have been as off base as the idea that all women should ever attempt to do is give birth, wax floors, and watch soaps all day?

I did not like asking myself these questions. I do not like being on the "wrong" side of an issue.

But that is where I am. No longer politically correct, or ideologically pure.

At least I am not alone. Like me, other women who have achieved varying degrees of success are also questioning the tenets of their faith. Trying to redefine and reinterpret success in a way that will permit women to incorporate the so-called "feminine" aspects of themselves into a healthier adult life.

Not that we are sure this can be done.

But it behooves us to try.

"I think we are perceiving a real change in attitude," Kate tells me. She is twenty-nine, married, and a writer for a morning television show in New York. Before joining the show a year ago she was a successful freelance writer, work she continues to do. She has also published two books, one nonfiction, one fiction, with a third due soon.

"At first women were forced to go after success on men's terms alone, because they were the only terms available. We had to grab whatever we could and maneuver our way in and prove we could do it, prove that we could handle whatever they chose to throw at us, and we could do it as well as, or better than, any man could.

"Now that women have proven their abilities and done their jobs without falling apart, I think women in their late twenties and thirties are looking around and asking questions all over again, questions about goals and directions and what's really important to them.

"When the women's movement started up, it was led in part by women who were married and had children and they were mostly housewives. Of course there are notable exceptions to that, Gloria Steinem for instance. But the movement really hit home and talked to women who were bored with their lives, or women who lived the dream of marriage and husband and children and found it lacking. Or women who were forced by divorce to go back to work and who discovered that they weren't qualified to do anything, they didn't have experience, and what work they could get didn't pay anything at all. Those women were caught in a terrible bind, and they were very, very angry. Remember how angry they were?

"And so the whole tone of what followed was colored by their particular experiences and prejudices, and much of it was very negative. It was; don't get caught like I did. Don't be a bored, frumpy housewife chasing kids and driving car pools and waiting hand and foot on a husband. It stinks. Women can do better than that and they should do better than that, and the thing to do is to work. Otherwise you might end up on welfare, trying to make ends meet with food stamps, saddled with custody of the kids while your ex-husband joins Club Med and parties all weekend.

"Now, who could argue with the idea that women should work and earn a lot of money and be able to take care of themselves and their children? No one, really, because it's very reasonable, it's smart thinking and common sense.

"At the same time, because they didn't want to offend housewives and alienate such a large bloc of women, there was lots of talk about choices. The movement was going to free everyone to make choices. If you wanted to work, that was okay, if you preferred to stay at home, that's okay, too, just as long as you're not being forced to stay home by your husband or by a society that won't let you go to law school or medical school. The idea was, do whatever suits you best. We were even going to make it possible to trade places and change roles with men.

"And there was lots of talk, too, about how women should never set out to become like men, because their lives were just as rigid and sex-stereotyped as women's lives were. They were victims too. So we were all going to go off and join the labor force and really humanize it. Then everyone would be better off, men and women alike.

"By the mid-seventies, though, practically all pretense about choices and 'do what pleases you the most' was gone. People still said it occasionally, but they didn't mean it. Instead, everything was success, and success meant, climb the corporate ladder and get as close to the top as you possibly can. Push everything out of your life that might deter you, because most of those things don't matter very much anyway.

"You know, it's very easy for women who have been married and who have had children to lecture younger women who haven't, and tell them that marriage and motherhood are not what they are cracked up to be, and to say, don't be like me, profit from my bad example, go off and do something important, something that counts.

36

And let's face it, some of their examples were pretty bad, and I certainly wouldn't have wanted to grow up to be them.

"So I listened and I followed their advice and I called myself a feminist, and I still do. But I think that for most women a time comes when all this success and career obsession starts to become awfully hollow. I started to want marriage, and I started to think about children, and I was terrified to admit it. Partly because I was afraid my desires would be held over my head as proof that women shouldn't be allowed to work in the first place. But I got scared also because I realized that those women of twenty years ago were no longer talking to me, or about me, in the way I once believed they were. I got scared because I realized that they were so busy trying to get in and get their names on the door, that they never bothered to try to build a model for success that takes the fact that we are female into account. Instead, they built one that *denied* it. There's no provision anywhere that really allows us to integrate a significant working life with a significant personal life. We're faced with lousy choices all the time, which isn't comforting when you realize that you might be talking about something as fundamental as having a child, and that's a function which is the single most important thing that separates a woman's professional needs from a man's.

"I used to listen to critics of feminism say how women didn't know how to act like women anymore. I would think, great, because acting like a woman meant giggling and flirting and batting your eyelashes and deferring to men no matter what. Who wants to act like that?

"But I've thought about that quite a bit lately, and I wonder if those people meant something entirely different, something more basic, a kind of warning, almost. If we weren't smarter or more careful, we might make it very hard on ourselves in a different kind of way. Hard to get married and to have children after so many years of placing so much worth on work as the only way to become a worthwhile person. Hard to be appreciated, respected, really, unless you work at least forty hours a week, and bring home lots of money, as well as do everything else a woman is supposed to do. Now the title of your job affects, or reflects, really, the status of the man you're dating or the man you're married to, the same way a clean house and a good dinner was the measure of a woman's worth, and the man's status, years ago. In other words, we may have trapped ourselves into a new identity that has as many, if not more problems built into it than the traditional female role we all disliked so much.

"Now the measure of worth and the definition of a successful woman seems to be 'a person who works full time at a profession, earns good money, attends to her marriage, runs a home or pays someone else to do it for her, has kids but pays someone else to look after them, too.' I've started to think that it's a crazy definition, and I find myself questioning it all the time.

"What I'd really like to know is, what ever happened to all that talk about freedom and choice? All the conversation about choosing a life that suits you personally—not one that suits other women, or your boss, or the men you date, or the man you marry—seems to have just disappeared. What ever happened to those broader definitions of success we all used to talk about?"

There is something I forgot to mention about Kate. She has a particular interest in redefining herself, and success. She is three months' pregnant with her first child.

2

Anatomy and Destiny

Sometimes I feel the need for a child very, very strongly. I can feel my body crave pregnancy and I fantasize about it. But I could never be a single parent. So when I started to feel this need frequently, I sort of adopted two children of my friends, one who doesn't have a mother and one who doesn't have a father. Last Christmas I had them over for a tree-trimming party. We strung cranberries and popcorn and had a lovely time. I have a lot of love and affection to give and it needs an outlet. So I'm thinking of getting a kitten. Pets are a good way to fulfill this need to give and get affection.

G lance over her résumé and she qualifies for the label "successful." The school is Ivy League, the job has real power, the income is more than sufficient to live on more than well. She says her father is extremely successful, and he demanded as much from her. She complied. She identified with him, as so many successful women do, not her mother. But now she feels trapped by the life. I do not think she would describe herself as successful. Not anymore. Like Kate, she is looking for a larger meaning to the word and all it implies.

I have never had anything but a very precise definition of success. Where I come from, success means one thing. Achievement. Observable, rewardable, demonstrable achievement. Intangibles such as satisfaction from a task completed, or contentment from doing any job well, no matter how small, never seemed part of the term "successful." Success was something tangible, something I could lay my hands on and, in turn, lay my hands on its rewards.

So I began my quest for success at an early age—measured by report cards and teachers' comments, academic honors and award-winning essays, all leading, even in grade school, toward one thing. College admissions, strictly Ivy League variety. Which would lead, in turn, almost guaranteed, to success in a profession. Winnie the Pooh Goes to Harvard. Mary Poppins at Princeton. The Borrowers at Amherst.

In short, I came from an achievement- and success-oriented family, and like many other successful women, I identified with my very, very successful father. I absorbed his definitions with ease. They suited me. And he did not see success or achievement as a sex-linked phenomenon, something to be encouraged only in boys. You could say he treated me like a boy, I suppose. I always thought he treated me like a person, but I know now that we fit neatly into studies that have been done about professional women. I identified with him, and I tried to learn who to be at his knee. Literally. I attended my very first baseball spring training camp at age three. Going back on my own, twenty-plus years later, was like coming home.

And so I rolled along and did my work and my achievement was observable, demonstrable, and rewardable. In short, I was successful.

Until I started feeling terribly peculiar when I discovered that I wasn't a boy. Rephrase that. I discovered I had as much, if not more, in common with my mother. All along I'd known I wasn't a boy. Unisex clothes are fine, and there's something to be said for androgyny, but I think I got tired of having to say it, personally. All the time. I'd built my life on the assumption that I could just march along like my male role model, do the job, become successful and then even more so. I had brains, energy, some talent, didn't mind hard work, so why not? When you identify closely with someone and their way of life, you don't take time out to examine what differences might exist as well. I saw only the similarities. And my way of looking at things was reinforced by the women's movement. I was encouraged and supported in my identification with the men around me, not the women.

But the differences did catch up with me. Try as he might, my role model could do almost everything, but he could not get pregnant. He would never have to work during pregnancy, or take time off to have a child, or worry about a two-month maternity leave's affecting his career, or even deal with any questions about career versus marriage and parenthood. For him the two didn't conflict. For him becoming a full-time professional, a successful one, and *staying* one, was the normal and straightforward path. He worked hard and sacrificed plenty, but he did not have to split himself down the middle, or trade off between family and home. He's male.

But I'm not, so that's what I mean when I say that one

day I realized I wasn't a boy. I couldn't follow—I didn't want to follow—down to the last detail, and perhaps even some of the main outlines, his path.

Of course, this forms part of the successful women's pattern, too. A commonplace reaction, they tell me, that hits somewhere in the late twenties or early thirties, and that starts the mad scramble to try to get one's personal life into some kind of order. A personal life that may have some very different demands and requirements from a male's. And so, suddenly, the definition of success starts to change.

This is what I think about success now. Today. I think that when you toss away the rhetoric and push the manifestoes off the table top, there are very few women who do not define success primarily in terms of their personal lives. Primarily in terms of their marital status and their motherhood status. One or the other is absolutely necessary.

I have tried *not* to think this. I have denied it. Refused to believe it. Scorned it, fought it, refuted it.

And ultimately I was a liar. Not at first, but eventually. Carry me, kicking and screaming, to a new ideological position.

Most women do not really consider themselves successful until they have fulfilled all, or part, of the traditional, historical and cultural definitions of what it means—rightly or wrongly—to be female. There are things that have nothing at all to do with title and income and power. With recognition or fame. They have to do with marriage and childbearing. Without one or

45

both, most women do not really consider themselves successful. Even though they may *disagree* with, and *disapprove* of those narrow and restrictive definitions. This is an uncomfortable thing to admit.

Some Definitions by Women

• A successful woman is someone who is successful at life, not at a job.
• Someone who is earning good money at a job she likes, but has a family to come home to. A woman's personal life is far more important to her than it is to a man.
• The goal of a woman is always a husband and child. At least, always a husband. I think a successful woman is a Superwoman who has a husband, child, and a good job.
• I used to think it was having a great job, money, and some power. Now my success is my daughter. The rest is just work.
• A married woman who has a first-rate job.
• A successful woman is happy and at peace with herself. She accepts herself for whatever she is, and doesn't shred herself into little pieces.
• Success is money and professional recognition for a man. For a woman, a job is very important, but when the chips are down her identity as a wife or mother comes first.
• I'm supposed to say a working woman with a good

career. That's part of it. But things haven't changed that much. I think a woman has to be successful in her personal life to feel successful at all.

It is the first question I ask every woman I talk to. What is success, and what is a successful woman? Almost without exception they define success in the terms above, with consistent mention of personal lives. All of them are between twenty-six and forty. The lowest salary is $32,000 annually, and two of the women quoted here earn substantial six-figure incomes. Five are single. Four are married. Two are mothers. One is an investment banker, two are lawyers, another a magazine editor, still another a reporter. One owns her own company, which does over a million dollars in business a year. Two work in television production.

Notably absent are references to executive vice-presidencies, chairmanship of boards, or even being at the very top of their professions.

Notably present are what are often called "quality of life" issues. What others might label, in a derogatory way, typically female and romantic answers. Being at peace with yourself and the world. Being loved and in love. Husband, children, family, home. The kinds of answers that are no longer supposed to be popular. *Relevant.*

Career is included in most of their replies. This is a change. Some kind of change, but it is almost impossible to ascertain what that change really represents. A response to the economy and the necessity, ever increasing, for two-income families? A response to the divorce

47

rate that has forced women happily or otherwise, into the marketplace in order to survive? Or a measure of how the economic aspects of the male-female relationship are beginning to change? Verging finally on some understanding of the fact that when one adult is wholly dependent on another adult for all financial support, that dependence can do terrible things to a marriage. It seems to be less and less acceptable for women to be passed, as it were, from dependence on a father to dependence on a husband, like some child-women whose bodies pass puberty but whose minds, capabilities, and emotional lives remained locked in a nursery.

But despite the inclusion of a job in the definition of success, whether from economic need or personal desire, what those answers say overall is that the final and basic definition of a successful woman has not really changed very much. Something may have been added, but that something never replaces a man or children. If anything, a job merely enhances the possession of the other two.

Sigmund Freud is starting to creep in here. Something he once said, or wrote, keeps insinuating itself into my mind. One famous quote among so many, from someone whose impact is incalculable. "Anatomy is destiny," Freud wrote, paraphrasing Napoleon, of all people, in Contributions to the *Psychology of Love II,* found in Volume II of the standard edition of Sigmund Freud. Freud is actually talking about the conflict between sexual or instinctual life, and civilization—not about male and female differences and limitations—but the quote has taken on a life of its own and is applied to a far wider range of discussion than its original context implies. And so it is that phrase that begs to be written here.

Mention Freud in any context and he brings an automatic temperature rise to lots of people. Gritted teeth, anger, disdain, hate—and unyielding love and admiration too. Feminists in particular seem to hate Freud, and possibly with good reason, although I do not intend to enter into a discussion here about the cons, or pros, of vaginal versus clitoral orgasm, or even if both do, in fact, exist. Enough has been written already on this subject, by people far more qualified than I to discuss the merits of Freud.

The anatomy quote has been thrown around by anyone—men especially—who wants to "prove" that women have only one true purpose, one destiny, and one means to feel fulfilled, and that is through marriage and motherhood. That women must condition themselves to accept this role and find peace within it, and not "give in" to masculine leanings toward careers and achievement outside the home. So I understand why the phrase drives certain segments of the population crazy. Actually, it drives me crazy, too.

But I have to admit that it neatly distills something that I hear from other women. They don't use the phrase, and they don't categorize it quite so cleanly, but when you look at their definitions of success, it's present.

That's upsetting, to say the least, because I have spent at least fifteen years or so of my life denying that biology has much to do with anything at all. I have adopted the position that the presence or absence of a uterus has nothing to do with anything at all, ever.

I think I was wrong.

The presence of a uterus, the ability to carry and bear a child, has everything to do with how women define success and the difficult choices they make throughout their twenties and thirties.

The standing response to the biological question is to dismiss it and say it's a sociological phenomenon, the result of cultural and societal conditioning. Women care about motherhood and children only because society tells them they must; that they are less than female, abnormal, and masculine if they do not. (One thing I have never understood: how pointing out that something is sociological in origin, not biological, makes whatever's bothering you less real or less problematic. "Oh yes, sociological," one is meant to respond brightly, perhaps with a sage nod too. "That explains it. Well, I certainly won't feel that way anymore, will I. My, my.")

I am not sure that anyone can actually answer the biological/sociological debate, but one can explore to some degree the question of biological and sociological influences, and so I consult an expert who comes highly recommended to me. A woman with a private practice in New York, an assistant professor of clinical psychiatry at Albert Einstein College of Medicine, as well as an Assistant Dean of Training at the Post Graduate Center for Mental Health.

"Is anatomy destiny?" I ask her. "Is there any real

reason to believe that women behave differently on the basis of biology, not sociology?"

"Well, yes, there is," she says. "To some degree. First of all, women have rhythmicity."

"What's that?" I am afraid to pronounce the word; it sounds like lisp material.

"I mean quite simply that women are governed by a twenty-eight-day menstrual cycle and focus much more on their bodies and what their bodies are feeling than men do. They are more in tune with them and are also more exposed to primitive aspects of biology, such as their own blood every month. A colleague and I recently completed a study on little girls and their dreams, and their dreams were filled with timepieces, clocks, and watches. This doesn't occur in little boys. It's a physiologically based response in the girls."

"Is that all? It doesn't sound like much to go on."

"But it is. It's very significant. But I can give you more. Biology is destiny in the sense that there is a much stronger craving for pregnancy in females than there is the desire to impregnate women in males. Both women and men have a biological sex urge, but the pregnancy desire, the desire to reproduce, is much, much stronger in women.

"And then biology is destiny in the sense that age forty is just about the last chance a woman has to have a child. That time frame is very important. It starts to color every choice and every action that women make. Freud used the 'anatomy is destiny' phrase in a different context than male versus female, remember. But if we want to use it that way, then in his day, biology was literally destiny for women, and a pretty miserable one. Pregnancy and motherhood and being housebound were not choices women made, but were givens, and all that they were permitted to do.

"Today women have options about pregnancy and motherhood and work, and in that way Freud's phrase is already passé. Birth control, abortion, and career opportunities have steadily chipped away at Freud. But if you apply the phrase narrowly, to the biological urge to reproduce and how that urge affects women, then yes, I would say that it is as applicable today as it was when Freud first said it."

"Then you don't dismiss this desire to reproduce as something purely or mostly sociological? Could you even guess how much society complicates and obfuscates the issue?"

"That's a very difficult distinction to draw. Perhaps it's impossible to separate the two. It's safe to say that society exerts a pressure *beyond* the biological pressure. And women might feel less pressured, or rather, might feel more nearly complete as human beings—more successful, to use your term—when they are childless or spouseless without the constant emphasis society places on women having both. There is a very real, persistent belief that women are incomplete, lesser beings, and not really women, unless they have a child and often unless they have a man.

"Whatever a society's current attitudes towards women may be, certain things haven't changed. Social conventions change, but many of the fundamentals of life don't change at all. Women are now in the position of having more options concerning the way they live than ever before. Those are societal changes, and women's lives have altered significantly in just thirty years. But still, the basic biological or physiological needs that governed men and women a century or two centuries ago still govern them today.

"Women live longer. They can choose to have a child or children much later in life. They can choose to terminate an unwanted pregnancy, or postpone a birth until later. Or decide not to have children at all. But the cravings are still there, and the time allotted to women in which to reproduce has not changed. It is finite, a limited period of time. Men can reproduce until they die, and women cannot. They reach menopause and that is a key fact. Having this limitation, what is commonly referred to as a biological time bomb, placed on the shoulders of women is a problem, and one that men just don't have to face.

"So while there are many more options for women now, they still face age-old restrictions about themselves. What you come up with, finally, is a dilemma of great magnitude. I'd say it's the conflict of our times."

I had heard of her through several people, two of whom have been in analysis with her. She came highly recommended as a thoughtful and concerned person who does not cling to one sort of therapy or one school of thought in her attempt to help her patients.

She is very different from another woman I consult, a woman whose books are advertised in magazines, and whose name I culled from a magazine article that dealt in part with some of the problems women have trying to work full time and do other things as well. Unlike the first expert, who is not well known in a city that grades psychologists and psychiatrists the way Michelin grades restaurants, this woman has a reputation and a rating.

Her office is tastefully appointed, as they say, with a choice not only of couches, but also of seating arrangements for those who may prefer to sit up rather than lie down. She has worked hard to create a serene and expensive ambiance, with a judicious use of pastels, antiques, *objets,* and books. I decide that what I really want to find out from her is her decorator's name.

Our meeting does not go well. That is putting it politely. I explain my purpose. I would like to talk about biology versus sociology. About the kinds of stress women feel when confronted with the conflicts and choices between success and a decent personal life. About traditional femininity and newer definitions of what it means to be a woman, and how the new definitions may leave women feeling isolated and unfulfilled. And guilty for feeling that way. I realize these are complex topics, I tell her, ones that we could spend years discussing, but perhaps we could make some kind of headway in general terms. No, I don't think so. She is looking at me as if I have escaped from the institution she committed me to only that morning.

"I don't know what you're talking about. There is no conflict," she says firmly.

So I tell her some of the things that women have

shared with me in interviews. I explain that I felt some conflict that often seemed impossible to reconcile, that some women seem to feel trapped in ways completely different from their mothers.

"There is no conflict," she repeats. "Those women you're talking about just don't know what they want. They are scared, and weak. There is no conflict. What women have are options and choice now. They have almost unlimited opportunity to do anything they want. I don't see a conflict in that, do you?"

I look at her. Her face is impassive in the soft light. Her eyes reveal nothing. I am hoping that she has the manners to be treating me honestly and seriously, as a reporter, and not as if I am a patient with whom she has to play all sorts of games and practice all sorts of techniques in order to "help" me.

"I am here because I have a magazine article where you advise six women with this problem exactly." I hold up the article.

"Oh, that. I hate those magazines and those articles. They are silly and pointless, those women's magazines."

We are getting absolutely nowhere, and not fast. I should have thanked her then and there and left. But I am stubborn and I don't give up easily, especially when I have waited two whole months for this interview, for her first available free moment.

Perhaps if I can find out something about her as a person, I can find a better way to approach her, or at least understand why she is behaving this way with a total stranger who is trying to seek out expert opinion on topics she is supposed to be familiar with. So I ask her how and why she became a doctor.

She tells me she was a bored housewife, one who expended all her pent-up energy and intellect on cleansers and child care. Eventually she decided to attend medical school and become a psychiatrist. When she went back to school, her children were in elementary school and junior high.

So I begin to understand. There is no way, even with all her training and her credentials, that she can hear me. She is that other generation Kate talked about, the first wave, the ones who got marriage and children out of the way, so to speak, and fulfilled the traditional and very private desire to "be a woman" and then said, so what else is there?

I try to respect her for her achievement, for the energy and guts it took to walk into medical school at a time when women were not very welcome, and at an age where she stood out as well. But I can't. I don't have enough charity to accord her what she will not accord me.

I thank her for her time and leave. I am terribly upset. I have failed to connect and to make her empathize, even if she cannot completely understand. I am also upset because, for the first time, I am forced to acknowledge that the generation gap between women is much worse than I imagined. She cannot conceive of my plight, after what it took to go through medical school, to fight prejudices and help break down barriers so that women like me could become 40 percent of the freshman class in graduate school. What is wrong with me, she wonders. I have been offered incomparable opportunity and access with relative ease. Don't I know a gift when I see it?

I also understand that in some way I am a threat to her. I came in swinging a crowbar at her version of the truth. The safest and easiest thing she can do is to mock me, and to tell me that I am the problem, it is my particular weakness or failing that makes me feel so torn.

She is wrong, but she will never admit this.

And so I think once again about the woman I met who loves her job but is borrowing the children of her friends at Christmas in an effort to feel connected, and who considers buying a kitten to shower affection upon, and hopes in that way to mitigate some of the intense craving she feels to be pregnant. I come back to the fact that a variety of successful professional women in the early 1980s, women who are supposed to be so different and changed from their mothers and perhaps their grandmothers, sound remarkably like those women when they talk about themselves and their definitions of what it means to be successful.

This perplexes me because we are living in a world, or a culture anyway, that pretends this is no longer true, pretends that in twenty years women have radically reshaped and redefined themselves and their concepts of what it means to be a woman and how women gauge success.

I am not quite sure how we evolved into this particular political position where dichotomy rules the day.

I wonder too just how long large numbers of us will be able to maintain it.

A political position is the result, most often, of a firmly held moral or ethical belief. Politics in its purest form permits people to unite the moral or ethical with direct political action to translate beliefs into specific action or policy.

I see the early years of the women's movement that way—the nearly pure uniting of a moral position with political action.

Now I see the moral and the ethical questions divorced much too often from the political—moral and ethical questions of biology and reproduction, child care, and child development. I see the emotional life of women being squeezed onto a plane where the only consideration seems to be how to make society in general, and an employer in particular, responsible for child care and development, so that women can get on with their success—women whose only measure of worth is work, income, and the ability to get ahead.

A plane where other questions are considered unfashionable, if not in poor taste.

I juxtapose this with the trend toward single parenting, and I do not mean through divorce. I mean women without mates, women unable to find mates—professional women, as well as others of course, who have given ten or twelve or more years to a career and not much else, looking for fathers, visiting sperm banks, opting for artificial insemination, rather than remain childless and alone.

To me this speaks more eloquently to the question of

what is a successful woman, and to the question of how much real change has taken place in twenty years, than anything else. Far more than the latest Gallup poll about women in the work force, or numbers of two-income households.

Many outward trappings have changed. Some of these women feel capable of becoming single mothers only because they have a career and a good income to give them the support and the confidence that in the past came only through a spouse.

But the interior landscape, the emotional lives of women, seems not to have changed in the same way, but to have remained largely the same regarding the most basic definitions of self and success.

I do not see why this should be considered a negative thing.

The broader definition of success I am searching for will neither consign women to the home and dependence on men nor nail them to a cross of professionalism.

It's essential to find a way to incorporate all aspects of the female life into a healthy, workable whole.

Women must begin by permitting themselves to express honestly, and without shame or defensiveness, the desire to fulfill some traditionally female roles—without being accused of failure, weakness, or retreat into gutless femininity.

I do not think we are even close to doing that yet.

3

Success Schizophrenia

Q: After first term finals Anne finds herself at the top of her medical school class.

A: Aggressive, unmarried, wearing Oxford shoes and hair pulled back in a bun, she wears glasses and is terribly bright.

A: Anne starts proclaiming her surprise and joy. Her fellow classmates are so disgusted with her behavior that they jump on her in a body and beat her. She is maimed for life.

A: Anne will deliberately lower her academic standing the next term while she does all she can to help Carl. His grades come up and Anne soon drops out of medical school. They marry and he goes on in school while she raises their family.

From "Why Radcliffe Women Are Afraid of Success," *New York Times Magazine*

A selected group of women were given the above test. They were supplied with questions, known as "cues," and asked to provide an answer, to write a story or scenario based on the question. The three answers above are typical examples of the kind of responses women wrote.

The test was devised by Dr. Matina Horner, then a practicing psychologist and currently the president of Radcliffe College. Prior to Dr. Horner's landmark study, women were commonly thought to be afraid of failure, in the same way that men are often afraid of failure. But Dr. Horner disagreed with this analysis. She believed the abnormally high levels of anxiety that appeared on the standardized psychology tests and that accompanied women's desire to succeed, indicated something else. And so she created her own test, one she hoped would help to determine what women expected would *happen* to them if they reached high levels of achievement; what the consequences of this action would be for them. Men were also given the same test, with males substituted for women in the stories. For example, "John" would be substituted for "Anne" in the medical school cue. Fewer than 10 percent of the men Dr. Horner tested responded negatively to the cues. Not true for the women. As Dr. Horner wrote: "... in response to the successful-female cue, *eighty-five* per cent of the girls were disconcerted, troubled or confused by the cue. Unusual excellence in women was clearly associated for them with loss of femininity, social rejection, personal or societal destruction, or some combination of the above."

Dr. Horner was testing women who were predominantly of high intelligence, achievement-oriented, and from families where achievement was encouraged and highly prized. From her study she developed a theory known as the "motive to avoid success." She continued this work (the first test was done in the mid-sixties) and several years later could still conclude: "... men and women tested over the past seven years still tend to evaluate themselves and behave in ways consistent with the dominant stereotype that says competition, independence, competence, intellectual achievement and leadership reflect positively on masculinity but are basically inconsistent or in conflict with femininity. . . . Thus, despite the fact that we have a culture and an educational system that ostensibly encourages and prepares young men and women identically for careers, the data indicate that social, and even more importantly, informal psychological barriers rooted in this image really limit the opportunities to men. ... Despite the emphasis on a new freedom for women, particularly since the mid-sixties, negative attitudes expressed toward and about successful women have remained high and perhaps even increased and intensified among both male and female subjects."

I mention that article for two reasons. I read it when I was in high school and I never forgot it. It was burned on my consciousness. Everyone I knew read it. Everyone was horrified by it. And everyone identified with it. It was sad, awful and true. We already knew it. The question was, would it be possible to overcome what we knew was wrong intellectually but felt so strongly emotionally? It had to be. The solution was to ignore your feelings, suppress your informal psychological barriers and get out there and do it. Compete. Succeed. Once enough women did it the problem wouldn't be there anymore, would it? Women wouldn't feel that way anymore, and neither would men feel negatively about women and success.

The other reason why I mention it is that I am fascinated by the way in which Dr. Horner's findings seem to have just faded away, disappeared as if what she discovered is not *relevant*. In little more than ten years society has managed to erase these inhibitions and prohibitions, and women and men are living and working together free from all former constraints.

Perhaps what fascinates me most of all is that many of the women lionized in this month's issue of *Savvy* or last month's *Fortune* are the very same age, of the very same time and experience as the women tested. They appear on television, these women, to talk about the joy of success and the beauty of achievement. They have it all, and do it all and perceive, so they say, no conflict, no problem with any of it.

I am skeptical, and not merely because of my own experiences. I am skeptical because the women Dr. Horner tested accurately perceived a very real problem. They were right to have high levels of anxiety. It's a legitimate response to a very legitimate fear.

And what I wonder is, why is it shoved under the carpet, this fear and this conflict, or kept in the back room like some aged and unwelcome relative no one wants her friends to meet? The problem exists. It seems more a question of when one chooses to face off against the reality and the anxiety. In college? At twenty-four? Or ten years into one's professional life?

"My job always makes me feel less feminine and less of a woman, even though my office has a fair number of women working there in positions of some power. I always feel like I'm overstepping my bounds, like I'm less desirable, a castrater, every time I issue an order. When you run around being in charge you feel masculine. So I try not to give too many orders, and that hurts me professionally. Or else I try to ask for things in a sweet, coy kind of way, and that makes me feel equally bad. It's a constant source of conflict for me. It makes me feel schizophrenic. I'm no longer an average female. I feel like a freak."

She has never heard of Dr. Horner. She was in junior

65

high school when the *Times* article appeared. She is twenty-six, a former business and economics major who invested in television production rather than banking. She lives in Los Angeles. I will call her Elizabeth. I describe the article and the conclusions of Dr. Horner and ask her, "Are women afraid of success?"

"They aren't afraid of certain aspects of it. They aren't afraid of making money or the kinds of glamorous, billboard stuff of success," she says. "But I do think that women are afraid of the sacrifice of time and personal life and lots of traditional things about being a woman.

"I do think most women start out sincerely wanting to be successful. They aren't just doing it because they're supposed to now, or to pass time between graduation from college and getting married. They begin to work and they work hard and get totally encompassed by the job and the success and their new image of themselves. At the same time, they begin to have a hard time balancing their professional lives with their personal lives, and most of the time it's the personal life that suffers. I know mine does. In the four years I've lived in L.A. I've made two friends, one at work and one outside work. I have little or no time to date, I have a hard time meeting people to date and not much energy for it when I do.

"Anyway, what starts to happen—and I see it a lot—is that when women get close to thirty or so, they do a 180-degree turn. They start asking themselves, *Now* what does this mean, to be successful? By that time they're no longer the hot young thing in the office, the successful young woman who's turning heads with her

66

ability and her dedication to work. They have a pretty good idea of what kind of satisfaction they get from their careers and where those careers will lead them in the future. And most of them are single. I'm single. Ever notice how there seem to be a very large number of single women in most offices who are terribly dedicated to their work? Sure, there are married women where I work, but they are far outnumbered by the large group of singles in their twenties and thirties.

"And so little by little their definition of success starts to change. It's pretty hard to perceive yourself as the great success you thought you were at twenty-six when you're thirty-three with no husband and no kids and maybe a negligible social life. Even in a place like L.A., where it's supposed to be okay to be anything at all."

"So do you think that being successful means giving up some part of being a woman?"

"I hate to even think about it, because yes, I think it does. I believe it someplace inside me, and so I deal with it by just refusing to think about it. I just *refuse*. I know that I can't continue doing this job, with its travel and long hours and overnight editing sessions and hope also to get married and have children. I can't give half to them and half to my work. I think it's physically and emotionally impossible. That way, I won't be successful at either one. And I won't feel successful if all my life is work."

"So what will you do? Where will you be in ten years?"

"Oh God, at thirty-six? That's so hard to answer. I don't know, but I can say this. The way I define success has already begun to change, perhaps because I've worked and gotten a great deal of satisfaction and pride from what I do. Maybe that's all I needed. I look around at two women in my office, one near forty the other a little older, who are both single and have no life but their jobs. They are the butts of cruelties and jokes, which is awful, but it wouldn't be so bad if they were happy or had what they wanted. They don't. I can see how I'll be treated in a few years if I don't have a solid personal life to bolster me at the office. So by the time I'm thirty-six I want to have a husband and a child and that's my definition of success at that time in my life. I don't see my way to being able to have all that and this job, too."

Because of her age, she has had that much more education and indoctrination about the dangers of the traditional female role and the importance of success. Yet she speaks as if it were ten or even twenty years ago. And she is echoed by another woman (I'll call her Carol) who is fourteen years her senior. Carol owns her own business, a successful firm connected with advertising. She is married and is the mother of two small children.

"I think women are very afraid of success. Particularly single women. It's very, very hard to be a single successful woman, no less hard now than it was years ago. I can remember lying to men at parties when I was single. I would never tell them I owned my own business. I felt if I told them the truth they would shrink from me and retreat. Silly, I guess.

68

"For women, success means sacrifice, even with a totally supportive Mr. Right around all the time. Successful women are caught in a bind. They have divided goals and so they have a divided self, divided between the personal and the professional, and that makes life very difficult. I think that men can have both a personal and professional life without this division and without feeling that they are torn in half, and that makes a very big difference for them.

"I was thirty-two when I got married. I really wanted children and I realized when I was thirty that I had better do something about it. Women really do have a biological clock ticking away and I think thirty is the turning point. Some women ride it out till their mid-thirties before they face it, but by then they are almost out of time. And from what I've seen, if they don't do something they wind up very sorry later on. I have several friends my age who, for all their successes, and all the goals they set and met professionally, are so lonely and unhappy. They don't think those goals are worth the way they feel now.

"I think it's very important for a woman to get out and earn a living right from the start. It's a terribly traumatic thing to be thirty-five or forty and have to go out and work for the first time. The old traditional role where women stayed home and lived through a man is not a good way to live.

"But one of the things I've learned is that past a certain point, because I am married and have two children, I cannot really compete with a man. In my line of work I have one real competitor right now, a male. He works from seven A.M. to ten at night at least five days a week. I can't do that. Not anymore. I just got a call from some investors in California who want to fly me out for a week to meet with them. I can't do that. I might be able to arrange it for two days. I do not have the same freedom a man in my position has. I recognize this and handle it as best as I can. It would be foolish to pretend that I have the time and the freedom to dedicate myself to my business the way a man does. Very few women do."

Sarah is a lawyer, a graduate of both an Ivy League university and law school. At thirty she is counsel to a major urban-development project. She is articulate and attractive, with lots of dark hair and cornflower-blue eyes, dramatic, eye-catching coloring. She is single.

"Through some process—and I'm not sure what that process is—successful women wind up feeling different from everyone else. From men, of course, and especially from other women who are less successful or who don't work at all. I have my job and it's a good one and I enjoy it, but I'm not dating anyone seriously now and it gets tougher and tougher to use my work as a substitute, or derive my sense of self-esteem from my job. And it gets harder and harder to face the social game and to try and meet men.

"I think the personal lives of our generation screws up so much for all of us because we have such strong dual expectations. You'd better be successful, woman, but you'd better bring home an adequate husband too.

Bring home the bacon, but bring home a man too. You wind up feeling schizophrenic, living a schizophrenic kind of life, where two sides of you are supposed to be equally strong and equally important, but never dominant at the same time."

"Are the two lives mutually exclusive?"

"They shouldn't be. We've been brought up to believe they aren't. That they don't *have* to be. I don't even want to think they might be, but I have to admit that it feels like they are, too much of the time."

She is not "aggressive." Nor does she wear Oxford shoes or pull her abundant hair back into a bun. Glasses do not obscure her eyes.

The thing is, she feels as if she looks that way. The classic portrait of a bluestocking. Even though her mirror reflects a slim woman in tailored and fashionable dress, attractive, professional, the compleat eighties woman, inside she knows there's an unfeminine, unattractive, terribly bright spinster fighting to get out.

I think most successful women have felt like that at some time.

Schizophrenic. Divided self. Torn in half. Not exactly what the popular press conjures up when it investigates the status of successful women in America. But I hear these words, these descriptions, over and over again. It appears that actually becoming successful, taking the risk, winning out over the one set of barriers and restrictions against a woman's actual, physical presence and intellectual and emotional capabilities to do a job well, does not do much toward eliminating all the other prohibitions women feel.

I wonder if the analyst I consulted previously—the woman who was helpful—has found that the women she treats are afraid of success, even when they are successful, and do they have any legitimate reasons to be?

"Yes, they do have reason to be, and generally they are afraid of success," she responds immediately. "Women lose the sense of being safe when they become successful. It's easier to live when there is someone close to you who does better than you, or when there are a large number of people at work who have much greater responsibility and power than you. Women lose an important protective coloration that they have relied on when they become successful.

"Men approach competition toward a professional goal in much the same way they approach competition for a woman with other men. They use the same methods and tactics. They are parallel kinds of competition and success. But women do not see professional competition in the same way they perceive competition for men or male attention. They are two very separate things, and they use different tactics to achieve their goals.

"So it is twice as complicated for women to be successful and believe they are still attractive to the opposite sex. The tactics used for the latter cannot be used at work. Unlike men, women are forced to divide their energies and their identities into separate compartments, and to function constantly on two different levels.

"I would define a healthy female as actively receptive and nurturing in male-female personal relationships. Nurturing as you would an adult, not a baby or child. What is healthy in a private life does not offer much help to women in professional situations.

"But men perceive their role with women in a personal relationship as one of protection. This is the exact opposite of the way they must behave in competition with women at work. Work actively pits employees against each other in the battle for success and advancement, even though employees are constantly working together, even as partners. Men are terribly vulnerable to a competitive female, more so than to competitive males. Women are threats and dangerous, and therefore women receive constant attacks from men in the area where they are most vulnerable: their perceptions of themselves as women, as being feminine and desirable as well as competitive and successful. When you couple those attacks with the knowledge that women can't succeed professionally by some of the basic ways they've learned to relate to men, you have a huge internal conflict building inside women. The stress and the pressure of living with this conflict on a day-to-day basis is enormous."

"Do you think successful women feel masculine?"

"I'm sure some do, but my hunch is that the majority feel asexual rather than masculine. Asexual and uncomfortable. After all, neither women nor men have been

73

taught to be asexual, or encouraged to repress outward and obvious signs of their sexuality. In fact, the opposite is what we encourage."

"What about the fear that success means women forfeit some part, or all, of their identities as women?"

"Many women, in order to achieve real success in their professional lives, are forced to deny large parts of themselves. They have had to live with limited social lives or no social lives at all. It takes a great deal of emotional energy and a great deal of courage for women to develop a successful career. It takes the same kind of energy to develop a successful personal life and a successful relationship with one person. I see increasing evidence in my practice that many women simply do not have enough energy for both. I also see a great deal of frustration in these women because it's popular right now to say that these conflicts don't exist anymore, and my patients are living lives that are proof that the conflicts are very real. They have had to deny or repress many aspects of being female, and they have no personal life where they can act their femininity out.

"I also hear a lot about emptiness and isolation, women saying they feel isolated from other women as well as men, and describing their success as empty or hollow. In most cases the emptiness is what we call an intrapsychic defense against pain, and in the case of successful women, it most likely means that other emotional needs have been starved in the drive to succeed. This is especially true with women who have grown up believing that they must achieve, where success is fundamental to self-esteem and self-worth, where anything less means they have failed. When women grow up in this atmosphere and then have this reinforced by the women's movement, they often wind up in a situation that feels like the worst kind of trap imaginable, and it feels as if there is no way out."

If this conflict between one's sense of self as a success and sense of self as a female still exists, is it possible that it is less intense than it was ten years ago? I hand my torn and dog-eared copy of the Horner article to an account executive, aged thirty-five, from Seattle. Call her Susan. She reads the cue, and then three answers from women. Right away she dismisses the second story, the one in which Anne winds up maimed by her classmates.

"I'm not an expert but I think that kind of answer would be a real rarity today. The other two, well, I can see myself writing either one of those, given my mood and given what might have happened to me at work that week. Most women I know are very proud of themselves and their success, and they wouldn't know who they were if they didn't have an office or a title after their names.

"But if I'm going to be honest, I must admit that late at night sometimes, after work, when a group of us get together and start drinking and talking, we sort of shock ourselves by the things we say. None of us has been married and none of us has children, and all of us are terribly lonely and afraid that we'll stay this way the rest of our lives. We knock marriage, and we make fun of women who are housewives and we're really pretty nasty about them.

"We're really rather jealous of them in some way, very envious of what they have done with their lives, even though we say they've done nothing at all. I think what we're really afraid of is that our work will prevent us from ever being able to have what they have. We'll be too busy to find the time for anything else, or else we'll be rejected by men we care about because we offer less in terms of time and energy and attention than women with less demanding jobs or women who don't work at all. That's a very scary thought.

"I guess I'm sort of saying what this article says, aren't I? Jesus, I can't believe it. I thought I was way past that kind of thinking. I thought I knew better. I guess not. Come back in a few years, I might even write down the second answer."

That's doubtful.

But the reality of this conflict is not. Access in large numbers to the world of success doesn't solve the problem.

If anything, it may exacerbate it. Competition for jobs and men, both limited resources, is intense.

4

Modern Bride Meets the Female Eunuch

It's always been hard to be a single woman, but I think it's harder today than ever before, contrary to what most people say. It's harder because people seem to treat women with good jobs and briefcases as if they could have everything they could ever want, as if a professional identity is a substitute for a personal life. The problems of Superwoman and day care and how to have it all get all the attention, as if every woman between twenty-five and forty is busy trying to figure out how to balance a job, a husband, and a family. I know a few women like that, but most of the women I know are like me: single professionals who are lonely and frightened and feel as if they don't exist away from their jobs. Being a single professional woman today has the potential to be one of the loneliest, scariest, and emptiest existences imaginable.

Writing about the status of single women in any era means running the risk of descending into a quagmire of tired clichés, "B" movie dialogue, advice column rhetoric, general moaning, wailing, and breast-beating, and other not so attractive forms of expression.

On the other hand, the distaste for discussion of the difficulties of being single, the shying away from the topic as if it's germ-infested, always struck me as rather misogynist: another form of belittling women, and turning a very human concern—finding a mate—into a trite and desperate plight of one sex.

A world of difference exists among women in their attitudes toward marriage, and a world of difference exists between a segment of women whose goal in life is to "catch" a man, and other women for whom men and marriage are one of two or three goals in life, career and children being, perhaps, the other two.

But somehow, we treat all women the same way when marriage is the subject: as Nora Ephron says, there's nothing worse you can accuse a woman of today than the desire to get married. Especially in light of the fact that the women's movement has devoted much of its energy to decrying matrimony and exalting work and being single as the pinnacle of achievement and self-fulfillment.

So, like the woman quoted earlier, it's always amused me, in a rather bitter way, I suppose, to listen to the lip service paid to the glory of being a single professional woman, and how remaining single has been transformed practically overnight from a negative status—she can't catch a man—to a positive one—she has her work and doesn't want one.

With rare exceptions, only a woman who has never faced the special kind of loneliness and isolation that so often is endemic to the professional woman's life could ever believe that a woman who is successful in work feels automatically successful in life, or that the status of the single female has anything more than a thin veneer of panache and cachet.

In fact, there's a whole group of women now who seem to me to be faceless and voiceless, a group lost in the shuffle of the first wave of feminism and the current reaction to it. These women were born somewhere between 1947 and 1958, roughly, and they are the ones who speak eloquently about the discrepancies between the way people *say* single women are treated, and the way they really *are* treated.

These women are the first to make professionalism and career a key part of their identities, and success in the marketplace their primary goal. They didn't come to this decision in midlife, they weren't forced into it by a divorce and the need to earn money, nor did they choose to become successful because they were bored with housework or children, or both. As such, they are the first group to wander into territory over which there was much speculation, guesswork, controversy, and rhetoric, but very little real, hard daily experience. Uncharted territory. They are not Betty Friedan's generation, nor are they what *The New York Times* labels the "post-feminist" generation, twenty-two- and twenty-three-year-olds who can't seem to comprehend what all the bitterness and shouting and pain of the past two decades was about.

No, these women are a generation apart, using the term loosely, a class by themselves, the troublesome "middle children" of the women's movement. Raised partly in the traditional female way, with emphasis in the early years on marriage and motherhood and being the woman behind the man, with textbooks that showed men working and women caring for children and the home, but then, suddenly, raised too by the women's movement, deeply affected and transformed by it. And now they all sit around trying to figure out how to reconcile growing up reading *Modern Bride* magazine alongside *The Female Eunuch.*

We all had our consciousnesses raised, as they say,

and we based major decisions of our lives at an early age on the tenets of our new faith, and so imagine the utter emotional dislocation and disorientation these women feel when suddenly they experience intense fear, loneliness, and the growing desire to live their lives a little more the way their mothers do.

After all, nice as it is to come home to a spacious apartment or home that you alone can afford, the place is still echoing with emptiness. (Or roommates, ten years after you left your dorm, which makes you feel like an aging coed who hasn't made appropriate progress on the fast track.) Talk about that tired cliché "lonely at the top." You feel like a fool. You're just some $40,000- or $60,000-a-year professional, not a millionaire with offices in three countries, houses in six countries, and no one to share it with. But somehow that's the way it feels.

And the real creeping terror, of course, is that it will be *too late* for you to ever change the way things are. Career and success demand nearly all of your time and your energy. This is true for men, and it is especially true for women, who are busy not only doing their job but always trying to counter the overt and covert prejudices against them too. The conventional wisdom has promised you that as a successful professional you are infinitely more desirable than a mere secretary or "working woman." And by placing yourself in a profession in which you meet lots of men, all of whom are professionals too and outnumber the professional women at least two to one, meeting potential mates should be no problem.

Perhaps true, but more often untrue. Work is one way

to meet people, friends and lovers alike, but there are no guarantees. And having an affair with someone at the office can ruin a career more quickly than losing out on a major deal for your company that your boss was counting on.

And so life goes on, and the terror grows. You aren't meeting men, or if you are, it's not often. And when you do, they're the kind who say they want a lover or a wife with brains and a career, but if you scratch below that polite statement you find out that the career is fine as long as it's less important than his, earns less money, and you're available to him from five P.M. to nine the next morning, plus weekends. Even if he's busy. *He* knows your place, even if you don't.

And so there you are, name on the door, designer suits, expensive boots, more money than you ever dreamed of making—and somehow you wind up feeling like the sweetheart of Sigma Chi, too close to June graduation and no bridal gown in sight. You go to bed at night and get up in the morning feeling guilty and torn. You aren't supposed to feel this way. You have it all, don't you?

And perhaps most devastating, you're the only one who feels this way. Judging from the popular discussions going on around you in the media, no one has this problem anymore. No one wants to get married—no women, anyway—because they are too busy enjoying the fruits of twenty years' worth of trying to graduate from law school/medical school/business school—pick one, pick all. Labor liberates, right? How could you ever be the one to admit you have doubts, to put a chink in the armor of solidarity, to show a crack in the national facade, to say, "This kind of life is just as imbalanced as a life of no work"? That being single is no great treat past a certain age, because people still treat you as if you have something wrong with you, despite your job. That little has changed, really, in how single women are perceived and then treated, no matter how many spokeswomen for NOW get on TV with statistics and charts and proclaim otherwise?

Sure, it's always been difficult to be single past a certain age, and that age used to be younger. Twenty-four was the beginning of panic-button time. Poor Marjorie Morningstar, dumped by Noel Airman, used up, finished at twenty-three. But married, thank God, at twenty-four, to that nice lawyer, Milton Schwartz, just as Noel predicted she would be. Rest easy, everyone, Marjorie finally made a match.

An antiquated attitude, "they" tell you, and they aren't telling the truth. The age has just increased slightly. Today, twenty-seven starts the trouble zone, perhaps twenty-eight in the most liberal of social circles. But if a potential spouse isn't on the horizon by then, you're in big trouble. This is something we all know. We just don't talk about it anymore. It's in the worst possible taste to do so, after all that screaming and yelling and litigating for other more important things.

"I worry much more about fear of failure than fear of success," Sarah says. "Fear of failure means, What if I'm forty years old and still coming home to a one-bedroom apartment in Greenwich Village? What if I'm lonely, single, and miserable, as I am now, and not sharing my life with anyone then, either? Being a lawyer doesn't make me feel any better about myself anymore, not if it means I don't have a pesonal life because I was so damn busy being a lawyer.

"As it stands now, I don't have enough time or energy to do all my work, let alone the energy to face more disappointment and possible rejection in my social life. I look at older single women and say to myself, Oh no, that's not me, I just can't end up that way. But I'm beginning to wonder if I will. It's very scary.

"I think successful women miss out on a lot along the way. It never really occurred to me to look for a husband in college or law school. I was too busy working and having a good time, and I wasn't interested in getting married. All I wanted was to be a lawyer just like my father. In college I had boyfriends, and in law school all the guys just looked like predictable little-boy lawyers. I could see exactly what they'd be like in fifteen years and there was nothing very attractive about tying myself down so young, especially to one of them.

"But all of a sudden you wake up one day and you realize you aren't meeting many eligible men. Things start getting tougher all around than you ever imagined they could get. I suppose the lack of available men is good from one standpoint. It gives me lots of time for my career.

"But at the same time, because my personal life worries me so much now, I find that I can't throw myself into my work the way I used to. I have this feeling all the time that if I can just get married within the next two years, everything will be okay. I'll be okay.

"You know, Betty Friedan was right about how women should live from a political standpoint. But in reality, after doing it for enough years, I can't see that this is any way to live at all. When you're in your early twenties you base your life on those assumptions you made about women and success when you were growing up and going to college. Now I find myself trying to hang onto them for dear life and still believe in them, even though I have less and less reason to.

"A company I was counsel for merged with another company, and a lot of us were laid off in the merger. The men who lost their jobs would put their arms around me and say, 'Don't worry, Sarah, it doesn't matter. It's not a crisis for you. You'll get married.' They meant well and they thought they were comforting me. A part of me was outraged that men still thought that way, but another part of me said, Well, maybe they're right. Maybe that's all I do want now, after all I've been through and all I've done. It's a real pain in the ass to desegregate places, so to speak. I don't like being called 'honey,' I don't like being given a legal assignment because it's a 'good' one for a woman.

"What we all did was fight our way into their world and fool ourselves that we've made progress and that women have made great strides. We're kidding ourselves. The only thing that has changed is that women are out there in greater numbers, and that doesn't seem to be enough. No matter what you do, if you're female they get you every time, so women had better have something else in their lives besides the office."

I am working late one night at the office. Everyone tends to work late, since we are all young and inexperienced for our jobs and responsibilities, and we all feel it. We have a whole show in our hands and we are scared to death.

I'm wrestling with a boxing script. Nearly everyone in boxing seems crazy, and I have a story filled with competing boxing promoters all hurling insults and unsubstantiated charges of cheating and corruption at each other. People in boxing are notorious for doing this, and charges that would warrant a Justice Department Special Prosecutor in any other field are generally greeted with yawns of boredom in boxing. However, it is a messy story, potentially libelous, and I have company lawyers on my back, and I am working hard on it. But my work is suddenly interrupted by a coworker who comes in and sits down.

"I really feel sorry for you," she says sweetly.

My stomach lurches. Right away I assume I have done something wrong, made a mistake on the air for millions to watch, or committed some huge political gaffe that will send me and my fledgling career to Cannery Row. I hold my breath and wait to hear what I've done.

"I wouldn't want to be in your position for *anything,*" she continues. "Twenty-six and single and in the TV business. My God, do you know what they'll start to say about you soon? The attitude toward you and the other single women here? It's awful. Men are so cruel about single women your age and older." She pauses and smiles sweetly. Butter wouldn't melt in her mouth.

"I'm so glad I'm married. Even if I get divorced sometime, I'll still be in a better position than you. Divorce doesn't have a stigma anymore, and no one would be able to make cracks about me, or wonder if I'm gay or if there's anything wrong with me. But you single women sure have a bad time of it. Watch out for yourself, okay?"

Then, after a polite question about my work she was gone, as quietly as she arrived. The room looked the same, and so did I, but I felt as if a major physical disturbance had taken place.

What motivated her to say those things isn't really the point. But it may be an interesting aside, because one of the points women I've interviewed have made frequently is that it is other women, unfortunately, who seem far more concerned about the status of one's personal life than men at the office appear to be. That there seems to be some horrible kind of competition going on—not professional competition, but personal competition. Who's doing better away from the office. Who's dating and who isn't. Who's living with someone and who isn't. Who's married and who isn't. It's a little like a high school popularity contest, with the popular girls preening in front of the wallflowers, asking them if they've got a date for the prom when they already know the answer's no. Let's establish the fact right away that a woman without a gold band on her hand at the age of twenty-six, and no immediate prospects of one either, is a worthy object for ridicule, pity, and company jokes.

But what bothered me so much about what she said—besides its rudeness—was that I knew she had tapped a fundamental prejudice most men and women hold, and hold as dearly now as they did decades ago. A destructive attitude, a weapon that could be used and used effectively, over and over again, against any female in the office, but especially against the higher-ranking ones who do their jobs well and couldn't ever really be criticized to any degree on a professional level.

And it's the kind of insult or attack that is hard to cope with, no matter how much you know, objectively and intellectually, that it's ridiculous. It feeds into such complicated, only half-understood and deeply held perceptions of one's self as a female, a woman, a professional, a person. It covers everything in one quick chop to the neck.

A whole range of sexual harassments exist on the job, and many of them are well documented—the boss who comes on, the guy in the next office who tries to have an affair with you, for example. But there's a much more subtle form of emotional blackmail that single women are subjected to in the marketplace. I saw it constantly. I heard it constantly, from women and men, about other single women in the office. Some of the remarks were so cruel, so vile, they made my blood run cold.

And those remarks are hard to counteract. Witty rejoinders and snappy quips don't do the trick. So what women do is to deny any desire at all to get married. What, me marry? Never—it would take time away from reading my *Supreme Court Reporter,* or catching up on my stack of the *New England Journal of Medicine,* or doing that utterly scintillating interview with Reggie Jackson for the sixth or seventh time this year. Who needs love? Who needs commitment? Who needs marriage? We have our work.

Yes, one has one's work. As well as the growing fear that after years of fighting for promotion and recognition and money and power and success, one will actually wind up with nothing. Alone.

Andrea is a lawyer, a litigator for a New York firm, a graduate of an exclusive prep school, and Ivy League institutions. She was a scholarship student all the way, a black woman from New York's lower East Side, a prime example of someone who has benefited enormously from the civil rights movement and from the women's movement.

"There is a special isolation involved when you are a woman, a lawyer, and a black woman lawyer," she tells me. "The threat of not having anyone to share my life with is not a vague, bogeyman fear. I worry about it all the time. Being black puts a diffeent complexion on the whole problem, if you'll pardon the expression. There are not that many blacks, male or female, in my position. My peer group is very restricted, and I won't be meeting as many potential mates as a white woman in my position would.

"I don't ever regret my decision to become a lawyer and to pursue success on this level, to perhaps price myself out of a market in terms of men. There are worse things than being single, and one of them is being poor. But at the same time, I see the lack of personal life prey terribly on women I work with and women who are friends. My lack of personal life doesn't overwhelm me now, but I know that it's probably just a question of time before it does.

"I do feel awfully isolated most of the time, and lonely, too, although I often enjoy being alone and feel I have the inner resources to handle it. Some people don't.

"But last week I went to a movie with a friend and walked home alone afterward. I happened to see Dustin Hoffman on the street. It was no big deal, but I wanted to share it with someone immediately, not have to pick up the phone and call someone and wait to see if they were home, or busy or whatever. I got home and put the key into the lock and walked into a dark, empty apartment, and felt so terribly lonely. Not despairing, but just so lonely.

"I've started watching other women carefully now to see how they react and what they do about their lives, and what I see is that more and more of them are opting out as they get older and more settled in their careers. They make getting married a priority when they become concerned about the imbalance in their lives, and after that come children. There really does seem to be some kind of fundamental urge to reproduce in women, and also a desire to stay with that child and raise it, at least when the child is very young. I see it in my sister, and I see it in other women.

"And what I also see is that the choice for women is

basically one of staying in the system and being a professional in the fullest sense of the word, which means having next to no personal life, or opting out, either permanently or for several years, and taking the risk that your career will be very damaged when you return. But with our society the way it is, there is no real give in the system for women, all the talk about day care and quality time notwithstanding."

"Andrea, I have a question for you to answer. If you had to choose between a good and satisfying personal life, or a very successful professional life, which would you choose?"

"That's a hard question, because one can't really know what one would do unless actually faced with the choice. But I am sufficiently a victim of my own cultural conditioning. I would choose a personal life over my professional life. Make no mistake, it would cause me a great deal of anguish to do it. I have worked so hard to turn myself into a professional and a first-rate lawyer, and I have much more to learn and much more to do. To give that up would be very hard and would hurt deeply. But I would do it."

She is twenty-nine, and a Chicago-based stockbroker. She admits openly that she is now seriously husband-hunting, looking for another professional to marry and have a family with.

"I was dating a man who was real marriage material. He was in his mid-thirties, attractive, intelligent, and very successful. I thought we were having a nice evening, both of us talking about our work and about business, and then all of a sudden he started telling me that what he wants is an old-fashioned woman to be his wife, a woman who puts him and his career and his needs first.

"I didn't know what to say after that, and I never saw him again. It upset me and depressed me, because it wasn't the first time it's happened to me. It happens a lot.

"I feel like a performing seal when I'm with men," Lisa says. "Like a cute little toy they pull out of their pocket to display. 'Isn't she adorable, she has a great job and she makes lots of money and I'm so proud of her' are the kinds of things I hear them say to their friends.

"Sooner or later, though, they say very different things to me. My job takes up too much of my time, or I'm not available enough, or interested enough in them. I get called selfish a lot, too.

"Maybe I am—I don't really know anymore. I do know that I'm impossible sometimes, worse than my mother could ever be, acting dependent or typically female with men, almost like I'm trying to make up for the way I act at work. If a date asks me to choose a restaurant I'll do something dumb like say, 'I'm tired of being in charge—I'm a girl and you're the boy, so you decide, you're supposed to.'

"Since I've always been attracted to very aggressive, smart, articulate men, I always assumed they'd be attracted to me because I have many similar qualities and

I'm very successful. It doesn't work out that way, though, and I'm scared, just plain scared, that I'm never going to find someone or get married.

"I suppose that deep down I'm afraid that it's my success and my career that will prevent it. Whenever a study is done on the women executives it always turns out that absurdly high percentages of them never marry or have children, while the male executives are all married, sometimes more than once, and they all have kids. The women are always alone.

"It's all so confusing and scary, I really don't know what to make of it all, or how to behave anymore. I keep seeing myself in fifteen years loaded with money and working late every night in a gorgeous office because I don't have any other life. Oh God, what a horrible fate."

Coming of age in any era means being molded by certain attitudes and assumptions that hold sway in a key moment in time.

Women of my era came of age in a kind of twilight zone, maturing in a decade where they witnessed the breakdown and crack-up of the social and sexual order that appeared so solid, certain and safe when they were small girls watching "Father Knows Best," "The Adventures of Ozzie and Harriet," and "The Donna Reed Show."

Undoubtedly every generation feels itself special, or believes itself to be unique, to experience and participate in and witness life at a special time in history.

So perhaps I am foolish to feel that my era is special,

"chosen" in a rather bizarre, disorganized, and not very nice way.

Yet I cannot help but think it, and no group of women better illustrates the pathos of the female condition than the single professional woman of today.

They are unbearably poignant at times.

5

Division of Labors

About six months after I got married I invited a friend from my office home for dinner. We got there about an hour before my husband was due, so we had a drink and waited. When he arrived I made him a drink, too, and then cooked and served dinner. The next day she walked into my office, closed the door, and treated me to a diatribe about how disgusting it was to see me wait on my husband. She said I was one kind of woman at work and a different one at home, a fraud. She was really angry. At first I was insulted, but then I started to laugh. She got even angrier. She couldn't understand how superficial her judgment was, and that there are far more important ways of judging equality in a marriage. She's never been married, so she thinks that the person who cooks and cleans is a reliable yardstick. She has lots to learn.

As if it's some kind of virus or a disease, marriage gets thrust under microscopes. Specialists in every field dissect and analyze the state of our unions. Research is compiled, surveys conducted, results released. Marriage is dead or dying; alive and well; enjoying a rebirth; about to be replaced by newer, less formal ways of coupling.

Whatever conclusions the surveys reach, whatever the particular persuasion of the examiners, I'm always struck by the fact that sooner or later all the discussions and pronouncements seem to shrivel into one topic: the division of labor. If women work, leave the home to pursue a profession and to become successful, who will vacuum the rug? Who will ferry the dry cleaning, sauté the veal, rinse the radicchio, puree the pesto, and of course, who will wash the dirty dishes?

I don't care who washes the dishes anymore. I am not even sure it's so important.

Once upon a time I did. It was a burning issue. I thought the world, and marriage, turned on this question. Stomach in knots after every dinner, face frozen in an encouraging yet stern grin, I would gesture majestically down the length of the refectory table and then give a queenly nod in my husband's direction. It was the signal, his cue. Your turn, husband. I did worse, actually. I kept charts and mentally kept score. Wife five, husband two. What's going on here, mister? We made a deal. What am I, your maid?

Now I think the only thing worse than doing the dishes is arguing about who's going to wash them.

I guess I don't sweat it so much anymore because I finally relinquished the feminist marriage fantasy. When I jettisoned that, I had to toss out the cardboard Romeo who went along with it.

This Romeo is a new kind of romantic figure. Dashing and gallant in an eighties sort of way. Attractive, intelligent, an impeccable dresser. Custom suits and shirts, silk ties. Luscious and mouth-watering down to the very tip of his leather goods. A professional man who earns plenty of money. Masculine, strong, independent, ambitious, assertive, in control and nobody's fool.

Still, he needs one woman badly—you, naturally— and he's very willing to admit his need. He's committed to his work and his success, but he's equally committed to his wife's career. They share everything. Housework is a fifty-fifty split down the middle, and she doesn't even have to ask. He can cook and loves to. On the

97

nights when they aren't sharing the cooking chores, chatting cosily in their country kitchen as they work, he's happy to cook the meals. As for the children? He's the first to leap out of bed to feed the baby, change the diapers, silence the cries, offer the comfort. He's in touch with himself, his wife, his kids, his world. He can express doubt, insecurity, fear, and best of all, he can cry! He's also the perfect lover, and he hates anything that smacks of sexism, chauvinism, or crude macho behavior. In short, he's the answer to prayers, a living dream.

I admit he sounds delightful, but he also sounds like a latter-twentieth-century white knight. He owes his roots directly to the tall, dark, square-jawed, ruggedly handsome hero of Gothic romances. The man who, against all expectations, pressures, and odds, offers Thornfield Hall to dowdy, plain Jane Eyre instead of the sultry, glamorous Miss Ingram.

This guy fascinates me, this Heathcliff in Ted Lapidus clothing, because he's a creation of women who pride themselves on their hard-headed, pragmatic, and unsentimental approach to analyzing and redefining the male-female relationship. It's ironic that in doing so, the eighties male often bears a strong resemblance to a wimp.

In the same way that I wonder why cardboard Romeos are so necessary, I wonder why it's become impossible to take a pragmatic look at marriage, and the things women have to gain by getting married. As an institution marriage has definite drawbacks, but it also offers much that women can use to their advantage. But no marriage is going to ever provide any woman with much of anything if some of the ideals of the perfect relationship don't bend, and if certain politically correct attitudes don't take a back seat at times. Women need to be able to balance the need and desire to marry with a need for an identity outside marriage—not demand that everything, now, from this day forward, be conducted as if one is living a magazine profile on twenty perfect couples who do everything right.

If success means not just the ability to work, but the ability to love, and if women define success as much in terms of their relation to men, marriage, and motherhood as they do in terms of work, then what is the point in pretending that marriage is no longer a viable bond, or that women—or men—have outgrown the need and desire to marry? Why persist in perceiving marriage only as something that degrades and destroys women?

Historically, marriage bonds may have represented literal bondage for women, license for men to keep them confined between kitchen and nursery, to deprive them of money and property, and leave them open to physical and sexual assault. Marriage abandoned women to suffer without legal redress because the law recognized no crime between husband and wife.

If that is all that marriage is, or can be, there's no case to make in favor of it. No woman in her right mind would subject herself to such treatment. It's an absolute wonder that any woman, given a choice, would amble down the aisle and wed.

But women with freedom of choice marry and they

continue to marry in ever greater numbers. So marriage must hold out the promise of something other than confinement, servility, crying babies, and dirty diapers.

What that promise is does differ a little among the women I spoke with, but they were remarkably uniform about the need to compromise between their romantic fantasies of marriage—fantasies fed since childhood—and their adult fantasies about the division of labor, and a different kind of romantic equality.

In other words, washing the dishes by definition becomes a shared chore between husband and wife. But none of the women held on too long to a demand for a fifty-fifty split from their Romeos.

"Without question our culture expects—no, wait—*demands* that women marry today as much as it demanded they marry fifty or a hundred years ago. Women themselves demand it. No matter how strong and independent a woman is, no matter how committed to a career, she can rarely fight off that demand. And why should she? I don't think any woman should remain single if she can avoid it. Psychologically marriage makes life much easier for women."

Alison is thirty-eight, married, and the mother of a five-year-old son. Born and raised in Mississippi, the eldest of three daughters, she is the only one to attend college and graduate, the only one with a career. Armed with a bachelor's degree in English from Ole Miss, she moved north to New York and wound up working in advertising in Philadelphia.

"I spent lots of years as a single professional, and I

still clearly remember my single self and the way I was treated, and I resent it as much today after six years of marriage as I did then.

"At first being single and building my career was fun; it was challenging and exciting and everything I'd dreamed about back in Mississippi. It was a good time for women, for getting jobs and getting promotions.

"I guess I started feeling uncomfortable after about four or five years of it. I started to feel threatened on every front, at work and in my social life. My perception of myself as a contented, dedicated professional started to crumble. I was raised on the idea that marriage is the culmination of experience, a happy ending as well as a new beginning, and I couldn't escape the feeling that my life was going nowhere. My income increased, my career progressed, and I felt like I was starring in the longest-running production of *Waiting for Godot*.

"As years passed at work, my colleagues began to give me a hard time about my lack of personal life. I tried to shrug it off, but it got reinforced everywhere, even by corporate attitudes. For instance, we had yearly sales conferences, one week out of town, and attendance was obligatory. They were set up for everyone to bring their spouses, with parties and entertainment every night, so that spouses would feel included by the corporation. Well, year after year, there I was, spouseless and dateless. It's rather hard to ask a date to take a week off and play escort. I grew to dread those conferences months in advance. Isn't that ridiculous? But they symbolized the epitome of the single life to me.

"As for dating, well, thanks to the sexual revolution, men expected to be slept with in exchange for a date. When I said 'Are you kidding?' the bullying would start. They'd say stupid things like 'What's the matter with you, you're no virgin, you're twenty-eight.' Or 'What's the big deal, you're supposed to be liberated,' or 'Oh, come on, you're not in high school anymore.' Well, obviously I had affairs and I wasn't a virgin, but these guys were talking about something different. If it had happened every once in a while I could've written it off and dismissed it by saying they were jerks. But this happened all the time with attractive, intelligent men who were just dripping All Ivy credentials.

"I couldn't take it. I withdrew for a while and stopped dating and started thinking. And I decided that the problem was that nothing at all had changed between men and women, not really. No matter what anyone said, or wrote, or proved by a survey or a national poll, as a single woman I was as illicit at work, socially, and in the eyes of the world as single women were decades ago. Unattached and available women, careers notwithstanding, are targets, free game, and still no better than whores.

"So that's why I believe that marriage is better for women psychologically, even though marriage has its share of problems and disappointments. A few years of fighting back at the way people treat single women and I was exhausted. Marriage seemed like a haven. And one of the things I value most about being married is the safety and constancy of sex within the confines of marriage. Sex without fear. When I make love to my husband, I know he's going to call me the next day, not disappear into thin air.

"I think there's nothing more dreadful than the single woman's feelings that she can never be herself without some kind of fear of reprisal. Single women, especially professional ones, are always on the defensive, always justifying or explaining something to someone. The presence of a man, or the absence of men. Assuring people that yes, she's thirty-one and single and just fine, thank you. They get overworked at the office because they have no husband or family to go home to, and people assume their life is their job.

"Marriage spares women this treatment. That's why it's better to marry. Single women just don't feel good about themselves after a while, and I don't know one who enjoys her success the way she'd like to.

"I'll go even further. I think women are better off married for a few years and then divorced. Divorce can be ugly, and the world may not treat divorced women very well, but it treats them with more respect than single women, even single women with impressive jobs and good incomes. It's wrong, but unfortunately I think it's true."

To a divorced woman with children who depends on insufficient alimony and child-support payments, who supplements that income with work that pays little, a woman fresh from the indignities of divorce court who must face the hurt and accusing eyes of her children, Alison's attitude must sound naive at best, or like crass stupidity at worst.

103

To women who got married young and gave birth early, who never had the chance at single life in a big city, a well-paying job and glamorous night life, Alison must sound like a fool who didn't know how to make the most of a great opportunity.

To others her belief that almost any marriage is better than none at all makes her a masochist, a weak and self-destructive woman whose self-image is still rooted too deeply in the need for a man, for approval, and who cares too much what society is thinking. Her attitude is precisely the one women are trying to get free of.

I suppose that, theoretically, all these points of view are "correct." Right. True. Circle one, circle all.

Yet Alison's points about marriage strike a chord. To me she makes sense, despite the fact that in theory I cringe too. I protest, perhaps too much, to myself. I am supposed to know too much about the relationship between men and women to agree. I am supposed to have seen too much already to ever accept her point of view.

Without question, women were raised, and probably still are, with too much emphasis on marriage, on acquiring an identity and self-esteem through a man. Searching for ways to build an identity as someone other than a wife or mother is the foundation on which the women's movement was built. The near-obsession with careers and success stems directly from the knowledge of just how destructive this emphasis on men and marriage can be.

But marriage wasn't Alison's big goal, nor did she drift aimlessly after college, hanging out on some Philly street corner waiting for Rocky Balboa to come to the

104

rescue. She found her own place, took direct responsibility for herself and for her career, and still wound up feeling empty.

Much energy has been expended by the women's movement to convince single women that they are complete, to bolster their self-images, to teach them how to treat themselves well, in the hope that if women could change their own image, the world would change its impression accordingly.

Women whose marriages failed, whose lives were too full of children and housework, who felt empty in a different way, stood up and proclaimed the joys of being alone and the liberation of work.

And the result of all this is that legitimate complaints and problems about marriage and commitment turned into a wholesale attack on marriage.

Marriage became synonymous with oppression.

Women who could frankly admit that work wasn't enough, that they sought marriage, women who chose to stay at home and raise children, all became victims of this attack. Marriage was something women wanted because they'd been brainwashed. They were victims of cultural conditioning, outmoded social attitudes, attitudes that not only should but could and would be overcome in time.

It's doubtful.

Marriage is, as anthropologists say, a rite of passage. It is one of the ultimate rites of passage, up there at the top of the batting order along with birth and death and childbearing. It exerts a powerful, almost mystical pull. It marks the passage between childhood and adulthood, and signals to the world, and to yourself, that you have taken your place in the community at large, that you will continue, or attempt to continue, the social order as you know it. Until you participate in the rite, perform the ritual of marriage, society treats you as if you are unfinished. As though airs of the child still linger about you. You are an outsider who is suspect, morally and sexually.

Immunity to these pressures and feelings is difficult to come by. Rare for women and for men.

Alison may talk about things that seem shallow on first reading, worrying about having a date to show off to coworkers, caring about how to tell off a creep who expects an evening in bed as his due after dinner and a movie.

But what she's really talking about runs much deeper. She's talking about taboos, how women who are single are still taboo in the eyes of the world and themselves. That marriage works to dispel the taboo, and to free women psychologically to pursue work, children, whatever it is they choose to dedicate their time to.

Alison may sound like a throwback to an earlier era best forgotten, or like a victim of her own timid conformity.

Perhaps. But to me, she also sounds like a realist.

I have always regarded Gloria Steinem as the utterly elegant exception that proves the rule.

Marianne is an engineer, aged thirty-one, married for little more than a year. She's the person who invited a friend from work home for dinner, only to be criticized the next day for the fact that she cooked and served dinner to her husband.

"Women have stayed remarkably united on questions of pay, hiring practices, work-oriented kinds of things. Nearly all the success we've had for women as a group has been in these areas. But we've been far less successful on the personal side, on dealing with love and marriage and how to work things out between men and women to some kind of mutual benefit.

"I think our trouble started when we persisted in looking at everything in terms of male versus female. I discovered that there were considerations in my life that just didn't fall easily into that kind of distinction. I learned that there were some things I wanted and needed that are part of the human condition and they just didn't belong as part of a power struggle between me and men.

"I think one of the main reasons I married, and one of the main reasons why people marry is that we are all terrified of being alone and feeling unconnected and unloved and unwanted. I know men and women who spend hours at work trying to line up plans for the evening because they can't face going home alone and spending an evening by themselves. On Monday they start planning for Saturday. They'll even plan New Year's parties in October, to make sure they have something to do that night. Everybody rushes madly to fill up their lives with work and play, family, friends, lovers, kids, pets, and hobbies, anything to latch onto to keep from confronting this awful loneliness too closely.

"And then along comes the women's movement to point out that marriage and men can really mean misery, as if we hadn't figured that one out already. Anyway, in its place they offer success, or success and marriage, the best of both worlds. And then they go ahead and set down the rules for how marriage is going to work if women work outside the home.

"Now, I'm not saying that married women should work full time and then do everything at home too. I'm not saying men shouldn't share, or be retrained into accepting housework and child care as part of their responsibilities.

"But two people working full time outside the home sets up immense conflicts within the home. I've had my share of them already, and I haven't been married that long—and it's painful. My husband considers himself enlightened and he doesn't believe that the house is my job. For two weeks he'll be great and then suddenly he'll look at our dishwasher as if he can't figure out why it was invented.

"What am I supposed to do? I remind him, I cajole, I ask, sometimes I yell. He apologizes, he knows he's wrong. But lots of the time I just do more than my fair share and I just do the work myself. I can't spend my married life grousing about how much I hate housework and how unfairly things work out sometimes. I can't come home from the office and treat my husband the way I treat my boss. It's not the same thing. I wouldn't get my boss a cup of coffee under any circumstances. If I act that way at home, I won't have a husband to come home to.

"I guess lots of women would criticize me for this, like my friend from work did. Well, I think women like her are the shortsighted ones, not me. I know where my own self-interest lies, and what kinds of compromises I have to make. I don't like some of them, but I make them. And so does every married working woman I know. I'm not prepared to be a single mother, I'm not prepared to live alone and have no one else to count on, so I'm prepared instead to swallow some of the just plain drudgery that comes with marriage and being female. I paid that kind of price to get where I am at work, and I pay a similar one at home sometimes too. I think it's worth it. Marriage is worth it."

See what I mean? Illicit women, taboos, fear of being alone, rites of passage, and still the talk nose-dives into who does the dishes and how often.

Housework symbolizes everything wrong with the old order and marriage. It represents everything dull, confining and boring about being married.

But it does not symbolize all of marriage. Marriage has drawbacks, and more important ones than dishpan hands. But getting married can, as Alison points out, grant freedom to women in complex emotional and psychological ways. It satisfies and fulfills the need for intimacy in ways other relationships can't. And it confirms a woman's identity as a female in ways only one other relationship can.

The unwillingness to admit this, to find ways and means for women to create successful personal lives built on their visions of themselves as females, as well as successful business lives, is the termite of the feminist soul.

The concept that a professional identity and success is a substitute for a female identity—consequently a marital and/or motherhood identity—ignores the basic need for companionship all people feel. It ignores the peculiarly female complications of the need and assumes that any differences between females and males are merely environmental, culturally programmed, solely the result of custom. It permits no consideration of the idea that men and women may have some fundamental psychological differences, as well as fundamental similarities. Worse, it presumes that males have it better. You know, the old free, white, and twenty-one (and male) stuff. It fosters the notion that if society just tears down some legal and social barriers, what follows is that women recreate themselves in the male image. As if by copying men in the professional world women can appropriate a male self-image in all aspects of their lives.

When legitimate questions about the role of women in society are carried to this extreme, when women live in a world where they are fearful and ashamed to admit that they want to marry or to have children, when women live in a world that indicts them for wanting to not only marry and have a child, but remain at home to oversee raising that child, then this new order doesn't offer much of an improvement over the old. The emotional climate of a woman's life today resembles the landscape of a war-torn country, where the ground is one huge minefield and every step a nightmare of choices, one misstep a disaster. A battleground where she must fight—morning, noon, and night, at the office and at home—with the men on the job and the men in her private life. It's an exhausting and impractical way to live.

The reality is that there's hardly a man or woman who will not sell out his/her loudly proclaimed ideals, turn his or her back on whatever stance has suited them, or sacrifice the so-called sexual politics of their cherished positions, to grab at a chance, however slim, at some kind of love, commitment, and shared experience. At marriage. And they will do it twice, three times, even four, in the hope that this time will finally be the right time, place, and person.

When you couple this with the way single women perceive themselves, and the way the world at large still reinforces that negative self-image, it's no wonder marriage is so vital to them.

And then, of course, there is the question of children.

"I decided to get married because I wanted a baby. Many women marry for that reason, and so do men, but they probably wouldn't admit it. It sounds too arrogant and egocentric even for a male, doesn't it?"

Marcia is a thirty-six-year-old executive for a chain of California food stores. She and her husband have a two-year-old daughter.

"I thought that getting married would be nice and I figured it would give me a feeling of stability that I didn't have and couldn't seem to find.

"But I was also a little reluctant to get married be-

111

cause most of the marriages I saw didn't look so happy. They were full of tension and power struggles, those kinds of things.

"Yet those very same married women in those marriages who were mothers seemed to me to be in an enviable position. Those women seemed to feel things I didn't, and know things I didn't know. I became miserably jealous of my friends who were mothers, so jealous that I would try and avoid them socially.

"I got married finally, and got pregnant about eight months later, and I got the first real picture of how dissatisfied I'd been with my life, and how badly I'd been treated by people before my marriage.

"Suddenly my family started paying real attention to me, not just the kind of polite attention I'd gotten for years: 'How's your job and how's your health?' I got real loving, supportive attention. Relatives came out of the woodwork to crochet me horrible little gifts for my home and my baby, all because I'd hooked up with a man whose name they couldn't remember. I had a wedding shower and got more crystal and china than I could use in a lifetime. There was a whole community out there just waiting to embrace me. It was very strange and very nice.

"I will admit that part of me was very angry about it, too. When did I need all this love and support—when I was thirty-three and engaged? No—I needed it ten years earlier, when I was starting out alone in my career and making barely enough money to pay rent and buy clothes, let alone a Cuisinart.

"But another part of me felt serene and satisfied and

at some kind of first real peace since my college days. It embarrassed me, but I couldn't help it. I was an independent career woman suddenly basking and reveling in this attention like a sorority girl.

"I'm not quite sure what happened when I crossed this imaginary line from professional to wife and mother, but people treated me with a new kind of respect. They took me seriously in a different way. It was as if I'd finally discovered the heart of the matter, or plugged into the basic rhythms of life.

"That's corny as hell, but I don't know how else to describe it. I'm not saying that I discovered that everything else I'd done was worthless or unimportant, that nothing can compare to getting married or having a baby. But I came to terms with the knowledge that I had a deep personal need for something more than my work, to feel part of a tradition and part of the timeless flow of life.

"I can't say that every woman should get married or that every woman should have a baby. But look at how many do, after years and years of work and being single, and after years of saying they'd never marry or get tied down with a kid. I said those things, too. And look at those women now. And look at me."

Marriage is supposed to be the ultimate statement of love. Love is remarkably absent from these conversations. So are romance, hearts and flowers, satin, lace, tulle, orange blossoms, and a blue garter.

I am not quite sure what this absence means.

I do know that love is implicit in everything these

113

women say about their perception of marriage and men. But it's as if that factor doesn't even need to be talked about. It's taken for granted. Of course you marry because you believe you love the guy. The real question is, why else do you marry? What else motivates you?

Marriage is surrounded by romantic trappings. It's smothered by them. By love at first sight, and being swept off one's feet, and gifts of flowers and rings, and just one look, that's all it took. Violins play, the world takes on a rosy hue, and you finally find yourself in another person.

Perhaps the important point these women make is that marriage is not a romantic bond. If you want romance, don't marry. Perhaps they are saying that romantic love is not unimportant, but less important than is often supposed, especially in the case of women. Romance is a necessary ingredient in marriage, as are attraction, affection, respect, and liking. But marriage is really a practical union of common interests, needs, and desires between two people at some time in their lives.

Recognizing this practicality, accepting the knowledge that no one marries simply for love and simply for romance, enables women to approach marriage in a different light, severed in some sense from old definitions and patterns of behavior in a marriage.

At the same time, it enables women to retain flexibility and the ability to compromise, especially when career and success form part of the marriage equation. If one accepts the fact that most women do not feel successful, no matter what their job or income, without at least experiencing marriage for some period of time, if

114

one can look at marriage in somewhat the same way that women are teaching themselves to look at careers, then women will be in a better and stronger position.

And dishwashing will finally resume its proper perspective in American life: a subject largely unworthy of debate.

6

The Managerial Mother

The whole topic of children, when to have one and how to live when we do, is tense. Sometimes it's as if we're talking about politics instead of a human being. Our talks turn into management-seminar parodies. How to divide up our time, how to have two careers, how to find time for the baby, how to find time for ourselves, and for each other. I don't want to spend the first few years of my child's life kicking him or her around like a political football, always arguing about whose turn it is to do what, the way couples fight over whose turn it is to clear the table and wash dishes. If housework used to be the battlefield, how to raise a child has replaced it. It's almost enough to make me never want to have a baby.

I f anatomy is destiny, at least in the limited sense of the female craving to become pregnant and give birth, and if most women ultimately define success in terms of the more traditional roles of marriage and motherhood, most women will eventually face a major conflict and be forced to come to terms with all sorts of warring identities, desires, and needs.

Mother. Those six letters form a word with a life of its own, with more definitions and connotations than I would sometimes care to contemplate. Mothers really take a beating, whether the beating is delivered by Philip Roth in *Portnoy's Complaint* or by the psychiatric establishment or by a generation of women themelves, who seem to feel comfortable attacking their mothers for not providing them with worthwhile "role" models because they did not become professionals but stayed at home.

Whatever a mother is—or isn't—a new figure is emerging to add to the folklore of centuries. She's the managerial mother: the final creation, or end product, of the male success ethic and the female determination to emulate it. She may have more in common with traditional definitions of fatherhood than any traditional definitions of motherhood.

"I'm very serious when I say that having a baby has become a political issue," says Beth, a thirty-six-year-old vice-president of a Texas-based firm. She and her husband have been married for ten years. She was not sure she wanted children and has only recently changed her mind. Now she is trying to conceive.

"I'm very scared to become a mother. I do want a child, but coming to terms with that desire has meant coming to terms with some very unpleasant realities and some surprising things I'm discovering about myself.

"For instance, I always assumed I'd want to keep working full time when I became a mother. I'd go back to work as soon as maternity leave was up, and find day care or a nurse, somebody reliable, to take care of the baby.

"Instead, I find myself wanting to leave work and stay at home with a baby for at least a year or so. Now that it's my turn to be a mother and it's my potential child I'm talking about, I really don't think day care is such a good idea. I don't think I could ever trust someone else to take care of my baby eight or more hours a day, five days a week, no matter how much individual attention they promise to my child. I can't escape the feeling that it is very important for a baby to have its mother, or its father if he's willing, available most of the time and be the principal influence on it so early in life.

"My husband isn't sure he agrees. He's a victim of the professional-wife syndrome, you know? His identity is wrapped up in my identity as an executive. He likes it, and he likes to brag about it, really, so when I tell him that the thought of being a mother and a full-time professional rather repulses me, it comes as kind of a shock. That's not what he's heard from me for the past ten years.

"He does try to understand, but he doesn't really, and why should he, after all the lecturing I've done? We have insane conversations where he shows me how we can work it out, and he starts to budget every minute of our lives and throw around the phrase 'quality time.' I hate that phrase.

"Or else he'll point to four women we know who are professional mothers and he'll say, 'See, we can do it too.' What he really means is, you can do it too, Beth. I have no doubt that he would be involved and supportive and a good father, but when you get down to the short strokes, it seems that a child is always more of the mother's responsibility. I see it clearly with those four women he's always pointing to.

"Men might know more than they used to, and be more willing to help when it comes to children, but they really don't seem to know all that much about babies and small children—how much hard work and time they take, and how much drudgery is involved. So part of me has to laugh when I listen to Paul talk about how we'll work it all out with both of us working full time.

"It makes perfect sense to him, you see, because all he's doing is describing the traditional father's role to me. You get up, say hello to the baby, have breakfast and leave. You come home at night and say hello and play with the child if it's awake and if not, you glance into the bedroom, give it a kiss, and see it in the morning. You see him on weekends. That's what being a father is. That's what his father did, that's what my father did. It worked out just fine, so it's not easy for him to understand when I say, 'Look, Paul, I don't want to be a father. That's your job. I want to be a mother. For a while, anyway.' "

"The kinds of careers women are pursuing now means that they must often play the role of a male parent, a reenactment of the traditional father persona," says my expert commentator. "See your child when you can, if you can, and explain your absences and lack of contact by telling your children that you are doing this work for *them* and for their future, so that they can have a nice life filled with good things. Also explain to your child that you enjoy working for yourself, too, but never overemphasize this at the risk of appearing uncaring and selfish.

"I have a large number of professional women in my practice and they don't seem to want to play this father role. If they have no choice and must continue working,

121

or if they simply want to continue working right after childbirth, they cut back on working as much as they possibly can get away with, and not on mothering. Many of my patients have taken two or three years out of their professional lives to become pregnant and give birth. Others, despite prior career commitments, just simply decided to stay at home. They felt it was the best answer for them and they did it.

"In fact, most of my patients with any kind of ambition or professional life are still forced to give up about two years of their working life in order to be mothers. That's as I find it from my experience in treating professionals.

"There is a tremendous amount of conflict for these women and a tremendous loss of identity when they give birth. They want to be two women, the professional they were before having a baby, and a woman who spends as much time with her child as she possibly can. In recognition of this conflict, women are moving much more slowly when it comes to getting pregnant. Many are trying to get somewhere economically and professionally first, so that they can duck in and out of a career, trying to make it possible to stop working for a year or two, and waiting until their mid-thirties to have their first and often only child. It's an extremely tough situation, no matter how you choose to work it out. Women are put in the position of having to make horrendous choices. And make no mistake, they are horrendous."

For me, the managerial mother started to become a real problem, and judging from the amount of press attention she gets, I'm not the only one confused and sometimes almost obsessed. My obsession dates back a few years, to around the time when professional women friends started to have children.

I sat back and tried to take some kind of objective look at how to work out my life as a television producer and a mother. Almost right away I knew, despite all attempts to rationalize, that it wasn't a question of finding the right management techniques, or choosing Motherhood Theory A over Motherhood Theory B, or even finding the right nanny or day care.

When I got done putting a good face on everything, I knew from the feeling in my stomach that there was no way I personally could justify having that job and a child at the same time. An infant/baby, perhaps even toddler child, anyway. Each solution, each scenario I created was more depressing than the one before it.

Scenario Number 1: I board American/United/Delta/ Pan Am bound for Vegas (boxing) or Detroit (auto racing) or Chicago (thoroughbred racing) or Tampa (spring training). I am carrying: one person (very small), one briefcase (bigger than person), one "carry-on" piece of luggage (bigger than briefcase and person) stuffed with all the *drek* of motherhood—Pampers, bottles, animal crackers, books, toys, Kleenex, Desitin, medicine, and of course I have forgotten something but I won't know what it is until we're 27,000 feet over Pennsylvania, and the baby is screaming for whatever it is that I don't have. Meanwhile I am trying to hold a last-minute production meeting to explain the gist of the story to the crew, dictating a shot list to the cameraman (who hates kids of any age) and the story line to the production assistant, while trying to amuse the baby, who, since it is my kid, is yelping in mortal terror because it hates flying as much as, maybe more than, its mother, who is a complete basket case the moment her eyes catch a glimpse of any vehicle that resembles a bird. Once we land (if we land), the hotel has forgotten to provide the crib (they promised us one) and the baby-sitter for six hours (All booked up, sorry) and so we all go traipsing off together to the stadium—where the baby throws up on my NBC blazer, and my PA yells at me because she warned me not to wear the blazer yet (she didn't get into TV to baby-sit, but she learns fast) and a group of players waiting to be interviewed look at me with such incredulity and contempt (kids belong in the stands, not on the field and come to think of it, woman, so do you) that I can't remember if the ERA in question is an amendment or an earned run average.

Scenario Number 2: Suffice it to say that this one concerns constant trips to the phone to check on the well-being of junior, and naturally I am told by husband/mother/sister/nurse/baby-sitter/whomever that the baby won't sleep/eat/stop screaming and crying/torturing the dog and how could I possibly expect anyone in their right mind to sit for this brat and what in God's name had I done wrong to produce such a dreadful little wretch?

I cannot yet speak from personal experience, only from observation, contemplation, and a knowledge of my own character; and perhaps things wouldn't have worked out that way. But once I started thinking about the reality of a child, not some abstract little human who could be used to further a cause, like Beth I discovered more about myself than the fact that it wasn't a terrific idea to interview the L.A. Raiders with a baby on my hip. Peel away the layers of my rhetoric and what pops out, gibbering, is a very confused and torn person who says, huh, I dunno, and feels mildly paralyzed once a week.

It's easy to be Little Ms. Know-it-all, armed with statistics and studies about motherhood and day care, marching in step with an army of young women who have all the answers and no children of their own. Definite fashions exist in motherhood, and theories come and go, tossed out eventually like a well cut and well worn garment that's finally seen one too many seasons. Right now, day care is *fashionable*—it is packaged and sold as something not only more than a necessity for women who work but as the best way to raise a child right from the start. At least, this is the message that I'm receiving from the parade of psychiatrists and child psychologists and child-care workers who appear on my television and in the pages of magazines and newspapers.

Day care is an absolute necessity; low-cost, on-site, company-sponsored day care. It's a necessity for women who have no choice about working, and it's one alternative for women who want to return to work immediately after giving birth.

At the same time, I have some doubts about day care as the perfect answer to every problem.

I cannot escape the feeling that if one chooses to have

a child, one assumes a burden of responsibility that should not, as a matter of course, be delegated to someone else on a full-time basis right from the start, on the grounds that the right to "fulfill" one's self through work must always be above all other considerations.

I am not sure that I would care to turn my child over to a stranger or strangers—with *credentials,* of course—and rely on them to teach and to mediate experience for my offspring at such an early age. There is time enough for that at nursery school, and kindergarten, and the rest of school and the rest of life. I certainly reject out of hand the popular notion that this is the *best* way to raise a child, and frankly, I shrink from the thinly disguised antifemale and antimother sentiment implicit in this attitude.

And then, one's worst and barely acknowledged fears—fears one dismisses quietly as "sick" and "paranoid"—surface abruptly when the Virginia McMartin Pre-School story breaks: alleged child abuse, sexual abuse, child pornography and more, in a popular and reputable day-care center. It is a depraved, vile, and corrupt story that emerged, and it is not a standard by which to judge day care. Yet it allegedly happened.

And so, what I am saying is: I no longer think I know what is right or best, do you? And if so, how can you be so sure? The jury is still out on this subject, and so I articulate my fear and doubt about "answers" that seem to have become gospel in a dangerously short period of time.

As I write these words, I feel like running to the mirror to see if I have turned into Phyllis Schlafly. I rush to clarify: I do not serve up the image of woman and mother as a self-sacrificing and self-denying ideal, or suggest that women who remain home with children are "good" and women who don't are "bad." Or that children raised by a parent at home for the early years are "happier" or "better" and children who aren't are "insecure" and "unhappy."

But if *choice* is the bottom line—women, success, and choices relating to the role of women today—I find myself leaning toward choosing what I know and the way I was raised. Instinctively I move toward it. I presume that I will have a measure of emotional and financial choice, a very middle class presumption. But then the whole topic of work versus motherhood is essentially a middle class one that also presumes a measure of choice.

And then, if choice is not my lot, I will survive my objections to day care, and my guilt, and so will my child. I may find myself unable to remain occupied by home and child. Then no doubt I will choose to do things differently.

Anyone who adheres to any political position simply because she/he once expressed a belief in that position is a fool.

Martha is a commercial banker. She has a one-year-old son. He has a baby-sitter every day.

"When I was interviewing women to take care of Mark I would sit there and think about how businessmen are always discussing the difficulties of hiring executives, what a delicate and important job it is, and so hard to choose the right man for the job.

127

"Can you imagine how important it is to find the right woman to take care of your child? Every day women make this decision, and it's a far more difficult and important one than the decisions those men are making. Not only did I have to find a woman whose style I approved of, I had to find a woman who approved of my style and my choices as well. And that's the hardest part of finding a baby-sitter. If the woman who takes care of your child disapproves of you as a mother because you work, or is resentful of the way you live, your social life and your economic position, then you have a real problem.

"Or if you, as a professional, believe someplace inside you that domestic help of any kind, but particularly women who earn a living as nursemaids, are less deserving of respect than you are, you also have a terrible problem on your hands. I was outraged when I listened to other women complain about their 'girls' wanting a salary of more than two hundred plus dollars a week, and treating them as if they have some nerve because they're unskilled labor, because *anyone* can take care of a baby.

"What hypocrites! They are the same women who will complain about the pink-collar ghetto, or publicly wail about the unfair lives of working-class women, or else they'll spearhead a movement at the office because women are paid less than most of the men, but in their own backyards they treat domestic help little better than slaves.

"Mark's baby-sitter makes my life possible, and I'm very grateful to her. She's invaluable. Priceless, actually.

She works harder taking care of him than I do every day at the office. I know because I take care of Mark every weekend and by Sunday night my husband and I are just exhausted.

"I've changed greatly since Mark was born. My priorities are completely different. I still enjoy my work and I take it seriously, but not in the same way I did before. When I'm at the office I don't think about Mark much during the day, and sometimes I don't even call home to see how he's doing. But I'm out of there at five every day and on my way home to Mark. There's nothing at work that's so important it can't wait until tomorrow. I feel rather sorry for those women whose careers are so demanding that they cannot walk away at five every day. It must be an awful feeling.

"I am more relaxed and happier now than ever before. There's a balance in my life that was absent before. Work is still important to me, but in a completely different way. It's healthier, and I'm healthier."

She reminds me of an experience I once had that I found less than ... healthy.

Several years ago I attended a women-in-communications conference to listen to a friend of mine make a speech. Lots of worthy women gathered for this event, and most of the conference was worthy but forgettable, except for one incident I remember clearly that occurred during one speech.

The speaker addressed herself to the conflict between motherhood and work and she told a story about herself and her daughter. An important sales meeting was

129

scheduled for the same day as her daughter's appearance in a school play. (You've heard this one, right? It has assumed mythic proportions already.) Well, she agonized and agonized, torn between her duty to her job and her duty as a mother. Finally she made her decision. She went to the sales meeting.

The place went wild. Cheering, applauding, whistling, stamping, hooraying. As if the delegation from the great state of Texas had just cast its votes and put the candidate over the top, I expected a band to strike up "Happy Days Are Here Again," balloons to cascade down, and posters of Roosevelt, Stevenson, and Kennedy to slide into place behind the podium.

While all this screaming was going on, I felt very strange. Not because I disagreed with the speaker's decision. Quite the contrary, I supported it.

But the intensity of the crowd reaction disturbed me. It far exceeded a natural, supportive response to the story and its moral. It reminded me of certain excessive fan responses I'd seen at so many sporting events, where fan identification with a team or a player far outstrips any kind of connection between an audience and performers. Those poor fools really believe it's *their* team. Then they wake up one morning to discover that the owner has packed up and moved the team to another city in exchange for a bigger, better, brand-new stadium with a dome. So much for the fans.

What I really wanted to know was, what was being cheered? Who was the good guy and who was the bad guy? The winner and the loser? Just who or what was routed, and who emerged victorious? The woman? Her

130

child? Or the entire male ethos? She really showed the world (read "men") that she's no sentimental sap about motherhood. She's got her priorities straight. She will do whatever needs to be done to prove her worth in the male marketplace. When the going gets tough, she gets going.

Perhaps most disturbing to me was my feeling that the crowd reaction was rife with overtones of self-hate. Not freedom or liberation, but dislike of the female self and the most fundamental expression of female experience: becoming a mother. Nothing brings it out more than the discussion of children. When to have them, whether to have them, and what to do with them once you do.

Playing the professional game the way men do seems to mean more than wearing pin-stripe suits or becoming conversant with Joe Theisman's pass-completion record. It seems to mean that women must adopt, and in some cases absorb and believe to some degree, male attitudes toward motherhood and children.

That attitude more often than not is one of boredom, disrespect, and sometimes barely concealed contempt. Mothers are not taken *seriously.* After all, anybody can be a mother. You don't need degrees, or law school, or an M.B.A. No one is more anonymous than the suburban mother, trailing through a supermarket, pushing a cart and towing a toddler. We know all about her from one glance: she has a station wagon, clips recipes from magazines, and if she ever had a brain, it's addled now. Her counterpart wheels an Aprica down city streets, clutching parcels, sometimes dropping them, dressed like a slob compared to the hordes of chic professional women who pass her by, giving her plenty of room. It could be contagious. People glance at women with small children, see right through them, and hurry to look at something else. Anything else, perhaps.

Naturally, all men and women do not feel this way. That is a danger of generalizing. But it is safe to say that despite the fact that our culture says it prizes motherhood, it acts in an opposite manner. Motherhood must be practiced away from the office. Motherhood must not be brought into the office. Children and pets not welcome. Housing developments are constructed that exclude couples with children. Restaurants frown upon them. Do it if you must, have your children, but isolate yourselves among other groups of women with small children, stay away until such time as their presence, and yours, will not trouble us.

It disturbs me to see professional women reinforcing this attitude. I wonder if it is the result of identifying for so long now with the successful male. If the key to success as they define it is to become as much like them as possible, then sooner or later I'm afraid that self-dislike becomes a byproduct of that identification. How much, of course, depends on the individual woman.

Los Angeles, March 21, 1984 (UPI): Mayor Dianne Feinstein has praised a court ruling that overturned a state law requiring reinstatement for women returning to jobs from maternity leave. . . .

"What we women have been saying all along is we want to be treated equally," Mrs. Feinstein said in a telephone interview earlier this week. "Now we have to put our money where our mouth is. What we were asking was to create a special group of workers that in essence is pregnant women and new mothers. I just don't happen to agree with that.

"... I believe that women have the choice," she said. "If they make the choice for career and children, there is no question there are problems. But I don't think the work market has to accommodate itself to women having children."

I don't happen to agree with the good mayor from San Francisco. Not only are her statements arrogant and cold, but they are utterly self-defeating for women. And she has an extremely peculiar definition of equality. Like so many vocal women whose position makes them so-called leaders of the movement, her whole approach is backwards. Her whole idea of equality seems to be based on doing things the way men have done them, the way men say they must be done. Men define the workplace, women adhere to men's definitions.

Her attitude makes a mockery of twenty years' worth of civil rights legislation that recognizes the fact that in order to achieve equality, a society must address itself to rectifying inequalities by treating certain groups as special-interest groups.

Pregnant women and new mothers are a special-interest group, and in order for them to be equal with their male counterparts in the workplace, they must be given treatment that permits them to carry children, give birth to them, care for them for some period of time, without losing their jobs. Without being punished for carrying on the species. And without placing a burden upon them of working till the delivery, and returning to work a week or two after birth.

Instead of using her position to demand decent treat-

133

ment and respect for mothers and small children, she uses her influence to echo men who throw up their hands and say, "The system can't accommodate working mothers, you either work or be a mother, don't ask me for special treatment, how can I conduct a business?"

Instead of trying to change the perception of motherhood and working mothers, she feeds all the negative stereotypes, and then calls what is left for women a *choice.*

It is disheartening enough to hear men reiterate how impossible it is to employ working mothers. To listen to women with power do the same strikes me as disgraceful.

No wonder the idea of being a working mother so often sounds so unappealing to so many. How much "choice" is there, really?

7

Corporate Women/ Corporate Mothers

I think we're being terribly misled about how much success women as a group have achieved and about how real that success actually is. I think there may be a bitter day of reckoning for many of us that's not too far off. A day where women will say, "I gave up my personal life, I destroyed my marriage, I didn't have children, I gave up this and I gave up that and what was it for? I still haven't been able to achieve the way men do, in the same arena they do, the way I was told I could." Let's face it: women are no longer disenfranchised, but we don't have anything like the power of the white male corporate establishment. I don't know if we'll ever acquire that kind of power, but if we do, it's not going to be anytime in the near future.

S he practices law. She admits being pleasantly surprised by the way her law firm treats her. She witnesses no overt acts of discrimination, nor is she sexually threatened or harassed. As a litigator she might have been shunted off the fast track into small-time work. That is not the case.

Still, Andrea instinctively knows that she and the women she works with are merely tolerated, not accepted. She fears this. She is tolerated because the law says she must be, and the law is enforced. She is tolerated, too, because fashion dictates the necessity of having a quota of women employees in positions of importance, sort of a proof of one's right and forward thinking, a measure of the partners' liberality and lack of sexism.

Andrea says that when she tells this to people, they

turn her off. They refuse to believe her, especially the men. They point to percentages of women hired, numbers of women in the graduating class at X law school or Y business school as proof they are right. They get angry, too, she says. Hostile. Sometimes rather nasty. If Andrea picked up a copy of *Fortune* magazine for April 1984 she probably feels vindicated. *Fortune* says she's right. Women aren't getting to the top. Women aren't getting past middle-management level. Why? The specific reasons are harder to pinpoint today than twenty years ago, but *Fortune* says, simply, it's discrimination, whether overt or covert, conscious or unconscious.

Once upon a time the women's movement believed that when enough women became professionals and executives, sexism at work would disappear just because enough women and men worked together on a daily basis and on a higher and equal level.

This is not so, according to a 1982 study sponsored by the Wellesley College Center for research on Women, and quoted by *Fortune:* researchers discovered that resistance to women managers *lowers* after a handful first become managers, but resistance *reappears* when the percentage increases to fifteen.

Women and men also believe—or assume—that men and women *manage* differently because they are raised differently. Boys are encouraged to assert themselves and lead, and they learn, through constant competition in sports, how to win, how to lose, and how to be a *team player.* Women are said to be at a terrible disadvantage in this area, not only because assertiveness and leader-

137

ship were never encouraged, but also because they have been systematically deprived of the team sports experience.

Not so, says the Wellesley study. Women performed well on tests that measured leadership and assertiveness, and they played well on management teams, despite their lack of Little League and All American experience.

This is a significant conclusion—one also reached by another, much larger study commissioned by a management training company—for several reasons.

Much of the movement advice and analysis of the past decades bemoaned the lack of female experience in organized sport, and it assumed that women would always be at a disadvantage in the corporation because of this lack. So they set out to correct it, by integrating Little League, and by explaining to women how men worked as a "team" by applying to their jobs what they'd learned on the field. By breaking it down and explaining it, feminist leaders hoped women could copy it, even if they hadn't grown up with it.

The female experts who glorify this athletic experience always seemed way out in left field to me. Did they ever read sports pages? Or attend Little League games and watch the way parents and coaches alike humiliated and bullied and criticized small children? Perhaps most importantly, did they really believe that the world of college and pro sports is one of idyllic and romantic cooperation and teamwork, all for the glory of competition?

Athletes are the male equivalent of the optimum female image. They are prized for their bodies and sometimes for their faces too. They live by selling their bodies, and age is the single greatest threat to their livelihood. Age is the enemy that will destroy their world. Athletes are owned by men, the team owners, who often parade and display them like so much meat. And any athlete can be discarded overnight, like a wife or mistress, thrown out on the slightest whim by a bored or dissatisfied owner, to be traded to another team or simply cut from the roster and left to sit around waiting for the phone to ring with the news that another team has picked him up.

Athletes live in the most insecure, constantly threatening world, where age or injury can finish them, and nowhere are a group of men working together so constantly and unmercifully exposed on an individual basis, despite the fact that they all pull together on a diamond or gridiron or court.

This is the experience women lack? Frankly, it's the kind of experience women are traditionally expert at, a performance to please a man. But women trying to enter a corporation have been made to feel insecure, deprived, and less than competent because they never played team sports.

If the two studies are correct, and women don't manage significantly differently from men, and they don't have trouble with leadership and assertiveness as was assumed, then where does that leave women and the corporation?

It's painful to have the underpinnings of twenty years of conventional wisdom knocked out from under us, yet that's what is happening.

139

Since the late sixties women have been counting on a change of heart—if not mind—from corporate America. It doesn't seem to be coming. Too many men, perhaps even most of them, do not want women around in positions of power and equality in great numbers. We are up against a blank wall.

Only when women can come to terms with this unyielding prejudice against them can they learn to *protect* themselves. And only then can they truly reckon the price of their success, and succeed, if that is what they are determined to do.

Circling warily, sniffing carefully, Andrea smelled this out, and sensed her constant vulnerability. The woods look calm and inviting, but she knows a predator lurks, menacing her, someplace inside the trees.

"I tried very hard to make it all look so easy, easy for me and easy for everyone I worked with, as if I had to make sure no one ever questioned the decision to put a woman into a high-ranking position, and to protect myself by having as few problems as possible," Corinne says. "My husband used to tell me I was wrong to do this. You put the value on it, he said, you let them know how much expertise it takes. You dictate your value. Don't let them do it. Well, he was right, but the sad thing is, I don't think it would have made any difference anyway."

Until recently Corinne was a highly placed television executive. After more than ten years with her corporation, and more than five in a key position, she was asked to leave. There were no real reasons given, and the company's move was unexpected.

"I always knew that this dislike and disdain for women in the corporation was there, somewhere, but I just closed my eyes to it and kept hoping it wasn't there for me. I couldn't believe it was. I got so busy with my life, which was my job, and I stopped thinking about it. I got along well with most of the people in the office, very well with my staff, and the key factor in my business, my ratings, were good. I guess I'm saying that I did my job and got results, I did what I was paid to do, and still it didn't matter. Little by little they've removed the highest-ranking women I worked with, women who were good, women who were threats, I guess, to male superiority and safety.

"The point of all this is not to catalog more abuses toward women in business—there's enough of that already. The point is, next time around I won't be lulled into the security of believing that times have changed, that I'm accepted, or that the quality of my work is all that counts, or that it makes no difference that I'm female. It makes all the difference in the world.

"My blood pressure soars when I read newspaper reports on the status of women, or watch programs where a handful of highly successful women are talking about the great strides women have made. I want them to tell the truth. Women aren't accepted, they aren't wanted, and women fight every step of the way, all day, every day. If women choose to go into the corporate arena they had better be prepared to be on trial about every aspect of their looks and their personality. Worst of all, women can't even tell half the time what's going on because men have become increasingly adept at hiding what they're feeling about women executives. So women had better be prepared to be fired for no discernible reason and to face sitting back and staring into a mirror and to go crazy asking themselves why. And then ultimately face the fact that, holy God, all you can come up with is that you're female.

"What happened to me also happened to two of my closest friends. It's been a bitter lesson for all of us. Six years ago I wouldn't have respected a woman who decided she'd had enough and stayed at home to have children. Now I do. Once you have squarely faced the realities, you're able to see your options more clearly. I'm no longer blinded by the romantic and material aspects of success. Life is too short to spend all your days maneuvering toward a chief-executive-officer post.

"Not that I've rejected corporate work. I haven't. I start a new job in two weeks with another big corporation. Nor would I advise women to give up, to quit trying to make it or be successful. We can't quit. But after my experience, I think it's time women were more honest about this subject and more truthful about the drawbacks and the unyielding prejudice towards them. I have a feeling there are too many of us out there lulled into the kind of false immunity I had."

It's easy to dismiss her tale. A whining, complaining, never-satisfied female. The kind who probably deserved to be fired, and now uses her sex as an excuse. There are

lots of those out there, using their femininity as the ultimate cop-out, right? It absolves them of all responsibility for themselves, their abilities, and their careers.

I can hear men saying that, but worse, I can hear
women saying it, too. I have heard women say it frequently. As my consulting analyst pointed out earlier,
the unfortunate thing about stories such as Corinne's is
that a problem that remains for all women is transformed into a problem that's personal, an individual
one. No longer a function of sex, and sexism, but a
function of personality. If she has a problem, it's her
fault. Haul out the corporate checklist. How did she
dress? Too feminine or too masculine? Too much
makeup or too little? Was she assertive, or aggressive
instead? Did she worry about people liking her instead
of respecting her? Did she play any team sports as a girl?
No? Well, that's the problem right there. She's not a
team player.

For so long now we have celebrated the superficial
and anointed the statistics, that when we're confronted
with anything that tells us differently, anything that
questions the belief that women have made such huge
strides in the corporate world, we attack the person.
She's a loser, she's not a good example, she's negative.
"Negative" is a description people seem to apply to any
statement of fact, or perception of a situation, that the
listener doesn't want to think about, let alone deal with.

Yet the fact remains that while we talk about equal
pay for equal work, or comparable pay for comparable
work, the latest statistics from the Census Bureau show
that the salary gap between men and women was wider

in 1980 than in 1970. The Reagan Justice Department decides to throw its muscle behind overturning the landmark Washington State comparable-pay suit, and women act surprised and outraged. Outrage is understandable, but surprise? Only women living in a dream world could be surprised.

So why is it "negative" or "whining" for female veterans of the corporate world to say quietly, "We are not welcome, not really. The boys have yet to emerge from the locker room. The clubhouse door is locked. Sure, they let us in for the team meeting, but they're all in uniform then. Rare is the woman who ever sees them with their pants down."

I mention this "negative" analysis, and permit a woman to tell her sad tale, not to add to more laments to the unedited directory of abuses women tolerate at the hands of the business world, but to draw attention to the pitfalls inherent in working in an atmosphere that merely tolerates one.

Some men and women thrive in the corporate atmosphere. Constant stress exhilarates them, daily battle energizes them. They love the intrigue, the politics, the outpointing and outmaneuvering competition from within as much as from without. Perhaps even more crucial, there are women who enjoy the kind of constant combat between men and women that takes place in business. Their juices flow at the challenge of trying to dispel and disprove myths about women, work, aggression, ambition, and competition that people cling to so strongly.

But there are other women who joined the corporation during the past fifteen years who do not thrive on such a warring scenario, and who no longer believe that war fought over the right to be there, one's sex, one's hormones, and one's uterus is productive battle.

If the problem women faced at one time was getting into the organization on any level other than clerical, now the problem is staying in, and rising significantly beyond an entry-level position. And the fundamental question is, is staying there worth the price?

As the *Fortune* article indicates, the idea that if women just bit the bullet and hung on, things would automatically come around in their favor simply isn't happening.

And so it takes a special kind of woman to handle the diverse kinds of pressures that success can bring. And most of us are rather average—not necessarily in terms of intelligence, creativity, capacity for work, or mental energy—but in terms of the emotional energies we have. Success by itself, with no considerations of discrimination, requires a huge commitment of emotional energy.

Couple this energy with the energy women siphon off proving how calm, efficient, unemotional, unfemale, and worthy of their opportunity to succeed they are and we see that women are asked to call up appalling reserves of energy to do their jobs. It's not impossible to do this, not unworthy, but very, very hard. Especially if a woman is interested in building any other kind of life for herself away from her office. If there are men with a vested interest in self-preservation who tell women that they cannot make it in the corporate world, there may be an equal number of women who spend their time advising other women to pursue career and success in the corporate world because things have really changed. Where doors were once closed, arms are now opened wide and welcoming.

Cant is not the sole property of males.

"I started my own business because I wanted to run my own life and not have to hassle with a corporation and corporate politics. So I left advertising and began my own free-lance business with a few hundred dollars and used my apartment as my office.

"Now my company does at least a million dollars a year, and people I meet make all sorts of assumptions about what kind of woman I am. Mostly they assume I have a real driving nature, an obsession to succeed, and that everyone has to be like that to succeed with their own business. Well, I don't have that kind of nature and I don't think it's necessary. Everything I've done in business I've done from what some might call a negative viewpoint. That is, I didn't want to stay in a corporation, so I figured out how to prevent that. I decided what kind of an income I needed and I worked hard enough to get it. Success itself was never my motivation."

On the surface she's the kind of woman worthy of a meaty and gushing profile in a publication that touts women executives. I think she's worthy of attention, too, but not for the same reasons others might. I respect her achievements, but I respect the directness with which she talks about women and success even more.

She sits chatting on the deck of her beach house, an

old boathouse really, with a few extra rooms knocked on. Little by little it's being dwarfed by three- and four-story modular constructions that are erupting up and down the Long Island coast. She is forty, married, the mother of two small children.

"I felt constantly put down as a female in a corporation," she says. "Constantly. Whether it was a direct put-down or the more subtle kind, it was always present. I remember the first time I asked for a raise. I was told I couldn't possibly need more money because eventually I'd get married." She smiles ruefully. "An old story, I guess. I didn't get married until my mid-thirties so I had quite a long wait ahead of me living on nothing, wouldn't you say?

"But that was the beginning of the end. After that I spent lots of time watching the women art directors and I didn't like what I saw, not in terms of how they were treated or what the job cost them personally, the kind of women they turned into. I couldn't handle the kinds of battles they fought and they seemed pointless because they all had to do with being female and the fighting never stopped. Eventually I decided I'd had enough, it wasn't for me, and I quit. After a year of travel I came back and started my own business.

"It was scary getting going, and getting where I am today was a lot of hard work combined with some luck. I didn't start out with any special training, just a B.A., and experience at an agency. I never went into business with the idea that I would be a huge success, or even that I had to be. All I did was set reasonable, short-term

147

goals, and when I reached them I'd set a few more and try again. I think that too many women who go into business for themselves, or who are afraid to try it, don't succeed because they think they have to do everything on a grand scale. They pay too much attention to businessmen who tell them they do, or to men who laugh at them and tell them they don't have a chance because they know nothing. Most of those men probably don't have the nerve to try it themselves. They work for corporations, and they can't stand the thought that some woman might try and succeed at something they were too scared to try.

"I'm glad I had corporate experience. Joining one for a few years is good training. But the corporation is a bad environment for many men, and a worse one for women. And for any woman who wants a child, or children, it's an impossible, inflexible situation. It's tough enough for me with two little ones and my own business, where I can make the rules, bring them to the office every day if I want to. Women who want personal lives have got to start looking for more flexible kinds of employment and more flexible routes for themselves. Branch out, take some risks, at least for a few years. You can always go back to the corporation. It just sits there, waiting."

Women are now approximately 53 percent of the labor force, and they now own almost one-fourth of the small businesses in this country. Ownership is increasing at a rate three times as fast as men's. Their total contribution to the economy is small, about 3 percent, and 45 percent of these businesses are in service industries, the traditional female labor ghetto.

But the experts say that our economy is slowly evolving from an industry-based economy to a service-based one, and for once women may actually be at the forefront of economic change.

Skeptics would say they are there for the "wrong" reasons: they didn't have the training to find work elsewhere, or they could not survive the corporate world, or because they chose to make money in areas where they felt talented, comfortable and in control, automatically limiting their own potential.

Yet they are there, in growing numbers, and they may profit from it more than one can imagine in the coming decades.

The only problem is that success in service areas is not accepted as true success, any more than motherhood is considered a worthy occupation today. This work is *less:* less prestigious, less remunerative, less glamorous, less powerful, less meaningful.

"Lesser in the eyes of men" is what is really being said. As if women cannot assign a value to themselves or define their own worth—even in work men are permitted to define a woman's self-esteem.

I think about this as I watch young professionals decorate their homes with handmade quilts that cost two weeks' pay or more, in middle-management jobs; or as I watch them scurry home from work at night, moving from catering establishment to catering establishment—one for pasta, another for chicken, a third for special coffee, the last for certain spices to season a salad. These

149

purchases are badges of status and taste, the marks of today's successful young professional, and tomorrow's corporate giants.

It seems to me that the women out there servicing this demand for designer food are very smart.

I would also call them very successful.

"Now you listen to me, young lady. I can't have a child. Only women can do that, that's a woman's job. If a working woman decides to have a baby, it's her choice and her problem. She can come back to work or stay home, I don't care what she does. But that baby is not corporation business. She can expect nothing from me. Don't tell me I have to find her a place to keep her child at little or no cost to her, because I don't. I run a business, not a nursery. It's bad enough I have to pay her while she's on leave. Now I have to provide nursemaids and nannies too? Absolutely not. After all, I can replace her with someone who isn't going to have a baby. That's my answer to you."

I should have asked him if he'd talked to Mayor Feinstein lately.

Or how he thought the Dodgers would finish this year.

Instead I broach the subject of day care with this man who is second in command of a *Fortune* "Top One Hundred" corporation. The mere mention of day care sends his blood pressure soaring. I can see it. Our conversation is conducted in vituperative hisses across a blond wood table at a chic and outrageously expensive Manhattan bistro. This is supposed to be a social occasion and I

150

have had the bad manners, the lack of breeding, to raise this topic. As he hisses at me his lips thin and his eyes narrow with contempt. He refers to me as "you people" and "people like you" more times than I can count. Had I been in the mood for nostalgia I might have savored my antiwar days, the last time I was consistently addressed as a bloc.

At any rate, the reason I brought up day care at a fashionable restaurant, in the middle of a social occasion, was because I wanted to take advantage of the opportunity to discuss something very important with an executive with the power to at least try and do something constructive about it. Right. Dumb. Naive. Adolescent. Wishful thinking. No way.

And I mention this episode not to delve into a long discussion of day care, but because I think this man is representative, a true symbol of the corporate attitude toward working mothers. Besides, I have heard much the same kinds of things from many men of all ages when this subject comes up. Where they once might have said it is not good policy to hire women because they marry, they now say, "Marriage is no problem, but what about children? We can't hire women because they'll want to have children."

What these men are really saying is that you can't invest in a woman professional because you will lose your investment when she has a baby. It's a statement based on a false premise about the investment a company makes when a male is hired.

Corporate executives seem to believe that when they hire a young man at twenty-two or twenty-five they can count on that young man's remaining an employee until retirement, thereby guaranteeing a return on their original investment.

Common sense alone tells one this isn't so. There are no such guarantees for males, or for females. All a company can ever hope for is that an employee will abide by the terms of a signed contract, and most young men do not receive contracts in the early years of their employment.

In fact, Tommy Jones may stay with his first company only long enough to get experience with which to bargain a new and better job with another firm. He will decamp for greener pastures as soon as possible. This is one of the fastest ways to career advancement and it's part of the way "they" play the corporate game of climbing up the corporate ladder—the game "we" don't know how to play.

I have worked for three corporations, and during my five-year tenure at one of them, I watched one man leave a top job to run another network, and leave that to become a sports league executive. I was recruited by NBC through a man who had been at another network for about ten years, where he had become a powerful producer and director, but he walked out the door and down the street to NBC when he saw a better opportunity for himself. After several years there, he left again, this time to form his own company.

The fact of the matter is that some corporate women will stay for a long period, or forever, and some will leave, whether it's to have children or because they have

152

found better employment. (A 1980 study by Catalyst, a nonprofit group involved with working women, indicated that out of 815 two-career families, 87 percent of new mothers returned to work within eight months.) But the point is that before one sits down to discuss options or day care or flextime or job-sharing, one must first analyze the way the structure works, and not be sidetracked by men, or women, who start from the premise that all corporate males act in one set, predictable manner throughout their professional lives, or that loyalty to a corporation is necessarily the way things really work.

Women also need to face squarely the fact that motherhood is not a rational topic for discussion in the eyes of most of the executives they wish to convert to their way of thinking.

"There is almost never any kind of coordinated corporate policy about working mothers. That's because these issues are not being dealt with on a high enough level. They remain in the hands of people in personnel or lower-level management. Right now the mentality is one of the company versus the family. It's possible to transform this generally negative and unresponsive attitude into a positive one if corporations would respond in a forthright way from the very highest level. Companies can become allies, not enemies, if they choose to."

I interviewed a man who runs a consulting firm designed to help working parents cope with the demands of their jobs, their children, and their lives. Since 1982 he has conducted seminars at corporations all over the northeast. He holds masters degrees in education and family health sciences, and has also received specialized psychiatric training in child development.

"A corporation brings me in for a variety of reasons," he tells me. "Most often I'm there because of one individual at the company who thinks it makes sense to talk about working parents and their problems.

"There's also an element of using me in lieu of providing day care or flextime. There's a growing perception that it's good for a company's image and it's good for employee expectations to talk, because it makes them feel their company cares about them. Quite frankly, I don't care what the motives are. In my own enlightened self-interest I just want to get in and talk to employees.

"As I see it, there are three basic needs a working mother has. The first is the physical need for child care. The second is the need for time, and to have increased personal control over that time. One of the most interesting things we've learned to date, those of us who specialize in family work, is that things like flextime and compressed work weeks do not lead to less stress for working mothers. Then the third need is confidence, the self-confidence to know that she can work and raise a child, and that's where I come in.

"Mothers cannot feel that they are sacrificing the family for work, or work for the family. I try to help them develop an awareness of their feelings and the skills for dealing with them and their children. Primarily they must convey to their children that they are working for money, self-esteem, and enjoyment, not as a means of rejecting them or wanting to get away from them or out of the house.

"Another thing I try to convey is that parents matter very much to children and the person or people who care for a child during the day do not replace a parent in the eyes of the child. They may become very fond of the person, perhaps even love them, but they do not replace the parent. And one indication of that is that children will save up all their rotten feelings for their parents, to share them at night when they come home with the person who matters most. Working mothers must expect this. The whole concept of quality time has just created another opportunity for women to feel guilty about working and leaving their children. Quality time should mean nothing more than being together and accepting each other as you find yourselves at the end of the day. It should never mean absence of conflict, the way it does now.

"Another dangerous theory I've seen develop is what I call the myth of separate worlds. It's recently been published in a new how-to manual. This theory says, Learn to compartmentalize. Don't take the office home with you and don't bring your family into the office. That's bad advice built on a negative concept. If something is wrong at the office you'll bring it home and vice-versa. That's human nature. When experts start advising people to compartmentalize, once again they're creating unrealistic expectations about the ability of people to cope. It creates guilt, fear, and resentment. What women have to do is learn different roles, not learn to be two different people. That's a key distinction.

155

"Exhaustion and guilt are the most widely held problems I've encountered in my work. Working mothers are dead tired all the time. They have no time, or very little free time, and they feel guilty that they are depriving either their children or themselves. As for fathers, the whole idea of being an equal at home is something most simply don't understand.

"Not only do they not understand it, they have no idea how to do it. If they think about it at all, they think in terms of traditional male jobs around the house, taking out the garbage or cleaning the garage. Yard work. They have no concept of what it means to be equal in terms of child care or running a home or doing any of the things women have traditionally done.

"This is very important, because if women go around believing that men will spend equal time with their children, or equal time working around the house, those women are in big trouble. I base that statement on many years of working with both mothers at home with children and mothers who work. Just because it is *desirable* for men to change and to do these things, and just because we give it publicity, that does not mean it's happening. Women who expect too much too soon will discover that their expectations cause anger, resentment, guilt—again a whole range of negative responses—in themselves and in their husbands. This doesn't mean that women should stop trying to change and improve things, or stop trying to reach the ideal, but they must be realistic about the effort it takes and the progress that can be made.

"So I would say that what I try to do is to help working mothers find ways to cope more effectively with everyday life, and to say to them, children are growing up differently today than we did. My purpose is not to reassure working mothers that what they are doing is okay. Psychologist types abound with all sorts of evidence to prove that whatever is popular at the moment, the way working mothers are, is okay.

"If we're going to be honest about this, then we're going to have to admit that the verdict on working mothers isn't in. We have given very little real attention to these problems and to the mental health of these women who are working, running homes, raising children, and keeping marriages going. So little that it's just astonishing.

"And there's one other factor here that disturbs me in the debate on this topic. We tend to dismiss the fact that generally speaking, women are anchored in their children in a way that fathers are not. It's very hard to judge whether this is biological, sociological, or some combination of the two. But they do relate differently, and I would have to say that fathers do not feel the same kind of responsibility toward their children that mothers do.

"That sounds horrible. I don't want to imply that there aren't lots of fathers who are very involved with their children. There are. But not involved in the same way that mothers are. I spend lots of time trying to encourage fathers to become more involved, and some do. But my experience indicates that women are anchored differently in their children, and it serves no purpose to

157

try and pretend that there are no differences between the two sexes just because it is more convenient to adopt that attitude.

"All of us who grew up in the sixties, who are starting families and thinking about starting them, should be trying to move into positions where we can use the family as a unifying force and a power for change. Not view it as a divisive thing that pits parents against children, wives against husbands, employees against companies, the way it is now. I hope what I do is a step in the right direction."

I like this man.

I was prepared to dislike or distrust him. My thought was: Here comes another expert, another male expert, waltzing into a corporation for one full day to tell women what to do. Typical. Wrong. And making money off it, too.

He is not like that at all. How refreshing to meet an expert whose expertise lies partially in his ability to admit he doesn't have all the answers. That he can't tell women they made a good choice or a bad one, a right one or a wrong one, but can only try to make things a little easier once the choice is made.

I would like to invite my expert to have lunch with my *Fortune* Top One Hundred executive. I would like to see if he can do any better than I did, if Mr. Executive would be more respectful and willing to listen to the dilemmas of working mothers and the corporate responsibility that should exist toward them, if they came from the mouth of a male.

Probably not. After all, this male works out of his home, often cares for his children, and is solidly rooted in an academic environment. I can see the executive look down his nose, nostrils flared, and hear him say, "Well, it's easy to see that you never met a payroll. Not a businessman, are you? What would I tell my stockholders?" and calling for the check shortly thereafter. Then he would depart with a polite "You'll excuse me, won't you, but some of us have to get back to the office."

At least it would have been a meeting with a top-level executive, instead of someone from personnel.

If not enough attention has been paid to the mental health of the corporate mother, perhaps even less has been paid to their corporate children. Not just babies and toddlers, but children. As my consultant pointed out quickly, there is always a psychologist or psychiatrist available to confirm the wisdom of whatever is fashionable at the moment. And psychologists do have a tendency to parade across my TV screen during news shows, advising new mothers on the latest in day care. One from Cornell Medical Center says day care is the best thing for kids since the passage of child labor laws. Another from Downstate Medical Center agrees. A third from Columbia Presbyterian warns solemnly that mothers who do not put their children into day-care centers risk harming them, by impeding their ability to learn independence, socialization, and negotiation. There is something wrong with all this: not with day care itself, but with a culture that hawks it the way vendors sell hot dogs at a ball game.

159

And day care for infants and toddlers is not the only problem. Where do children go, all of them, at all ages, from seven or eight in the morning till six or seven or eight at night? It's a problem that doesn't end with elementary school.

And so phone services are springing up across the country, a number for latchkey children to call during the hours they are home alone. Like many women, I have been so concerned about the day-care issue, corporate responsibility to provide it, my own firm belief in it warring with my doubts about it, that I have neglected to think about the older children.

So I dial a number in Pennsylvania to find out about one service and to speak with one of the women who started it back in 1982. She tells me the service was started in her living room one night, because the need for support services for mothers and children was so widespread in their college town community. The service operates during afternoon hours of the school year. About twenty volunteers man the phones, usually one at a time. They serve 5,500 elementary-aged school children, and average fifty-five calls a week. Fifty-one percent of the calls come from girls, 49 percent from boys. Thirty-three percent of the calls come from eight- and nine-year-olds.

They call because they are lonely, she tells me. Loneliness is the major problem for these kids. They also call because they are scared. Some call to talk about specific problems, or sex, or household maintenance.

"We try to focus on the needs of the children, to use a

reflective method of answering and talking to them," she explains. "We try to deal with the feelings of the child, not how we feel about what the child is saying. For example, if someone calls to say they got an 'A' on a test, we say, 'Boy, you must be so proud of yourself,' not 'I'm so proud of you.'

"Volunteers go through six or seven hours of training, mostly in how to listen. We have a Rolodex with an index of one hundred problems and different instructions or solutions for the problems matched for different ages. Everything from frozen pipes and sick pets to what to do if a child drops something made of glass. We might tell a five-year-old to cover it and keep away from it, but tell an eleven-year-old how to safely clean it up. And we always ask them what they think their parents would want them to do. We try to give them information for coping."

I want to know how this woman feels about these children and their parents, how she responds emotionally to this. She is reluctant to tell me.

"I try to leave my personal feelings out when I discuss this; I won't say it's good for children to be alone, nor will I say it's bad. I'm very pleased to be able to help meet a need and be helpful to children who need us. My reaction varies, of course, depending on what a child says when he or she calls."

I persist. Certainly she must have some opinion and reaction about lonely children.

"All right. I wouldn't want you to think that any of us believe that the phone is a substitute for one-on-one

161

care. This is not the number-one choice for any of us as the best way to raise children. It's not really a viable alternative, but it's the best we can offer and it does fill a need. But teaching children how to use a telephone, well, that's not the same thing as a person, is it?"

No, it isn't. But it is better than nothing at all.

8

Does Superwoman Really Have It All?

There is an ad for a women's magazine that features a woman called The Juggler. In the ad a woman of indeterminate age, somewhere between twenty-six and thirty-six, is kicking up one heel, throwing out her hands palms up, and wearing a positively vivacious expression. She is juggling three balls. In the first is a picture of a smiling little boy, oh, so proud of Mommy. A beaming and indulgent-looking husband sits in the second, and the third is filled with a bulging briefcase, the symbol of male power appropriated by women. Every time I see that ad, my stomach tightens. I'm a juggler, and it's nothing joyful, the way the ad pictures it. I'm sort of dragging all the time, I have no patience and a very short fuse, and I hardly ever see my four-year-old son. I have terrible guilt that tugs at me all the time, I have one role too many, and there isn't enough of me to go around. I live on the edge, I feel torn in half all the time, and frankly, I just don't know if it's worth it.

Perhaps it's not possible to pinpoint exactly when the term "Superwoman" entered our vernacular, but it's probably safe to say that by the mid-seventies this description of women was popular and commonplace, a catchword used to denote a woman who had her career, her husband, her children, her home, and managed all of them successfully—a woman who, in today's vernacular, "has it all" and "does it all."

"Having it all" and "doing it all" are supposedly the goals of the eighties woman, the ultimate achievement and proof that women are capable of doing anything and everything, and that they can find happiness and fulfillment in a multiplicity of roles.

This is a rather significant change in about a decade's time, because back in the early seventies the term "Superwoman" was less of a compliment and more of a tongue-in-cheek, rueful, and occasionally scornful way to describe women who were carrying huge loads with a thousand and one competing and conflicting interests, and never, ever enough time to themselves. In other words, Superwomen were to be respected, and admired, but not necessarily copied. Anyone with two eyes and modicum of common sense could see that these women for the most part were run ragged, and never had time to relax, let alone savor their achievements. It almost seemed at times as if the very things that were supposed to enhance their self-images and strengthen their self-esteem did exactly the opposite.

But something has happened in the intervening years, and I think it's more than the economy forcing women to work for a second income. What's happened is one of the most pervasive, most successful public-relations campaigns of all time: a media hype of massive proportions, spearheaded by a coterie of Superwomen aided by willing journalists anxious to proclaim a trend and anoint the new idol.

The reality of life as Superwoman hasn't changed in ten years or so. On-site, low-cost day care is not a national priority; the majority of husbands across the nation probably do not see the necessity of having dishpan hands and finger-painting sessions with toddlers, and the majority of workers in our country cannot afford much, or any, domestic help—let alone full-time or live-in household managers who relieve both working wives and husbands of much of the burden of household chores and child care.

But somehow this ideal woman has gotten the stamp

165

of approval. She glitters on her pedestal, a glamorous objet d'art, in much the same way a Marilyn Monroe glittered as a glamorous idol and prototype in a different era, that asked different things of women.

Idealization of any concept, any goal, is necessary up to a point. Women struggling to become something other than a homemaker and mother need to see and hear from successful women who struggled and made it into a different and wider world. But we may have moved way beyond that point now, into an area where the definition of a successful woman today—an eighties woman—is too far outside the reality of what is comfortable, possible, and feasible for most of us. Perhaps we have raised the stakes so high, rewritten the rule book so thoroughly, that most of us can't begin to emulate the ideal or conform to the new prototype.

It is easy for the most successful of women, many of them famous, to hold themselves up as women who have it all and do it all and therefore are models for the rest of us. They make good copy for newspapers and magazines, and even better guests on television talk shows. They dispense advice the way they might have dispensed coffee twenty years ago. A handful of them almost have secondary careers capitalizing on an issue that is ripe for exploitation. Their intentions may be good, their stories interesting, their advice noteworthy. But they are not the average Superwoman.

The woman who says she's short-tempered, guilty, and torn in half too much of the time is the "average" eighties woman. She is the decorating editor for a national magazine, and though her annual income is well

166

above the national average, and her job is a prestigious one, print journalism does not make people wealthy. She earns about forty thousand dollars a year and her husband earns much less, and they make their home in New York City, an expensive place to live to say the least, and they struggle to make ends meet on their combined incomes. A little over seven thousand dollars a year is automatically earmarked for their son's day-care center. His day-care tuition is higher than his kindergarten will be next year in a small private school.

I meet Jane at eight o'clock one evening in her office to do an interview. I assumed that this was a special arrangement, until she told me that she works until nine or ten almost every night. So I ask her to describe a typical day for me, and to tell me about the quality of her life.

"I'm up at six every morning during the week, or six-fifteen at the latest. After my coffee I shower and dress and do my hair and makeup. That takes some time, because image is important in my position, so I'm never able to go to work looking sloppy or even casual. My husband and son are both slow to wake up and get going in the morning, so I wake them up at about seven, and then spend the next ten minutes or so making sure they get up. My husband Michael takes care of himself in the morning once he's awake, but our son is my job. I get him up, dressed, fed, and we leave by quarter to eight, so he can be at the day-care center when it opens at eight. After that I go on to work. Michael's hours are more regular and more flexible than mine, so he picks Christopher up around five. I'm very lucky in that respect, because Michael is not only willing to take care of Chris, but his job allows him to. Michael is responsible for him almost all evening, every evening. He feeds him dinner and plays with him, and also makes dinner for himself and for me.

"I'm at work at eight-thirty and I spend an average of eleven or twelve hours a day here, excluding the commute to and from work, which probably takes an hour altogether, depending on the traffic. It takes much longer to get here in the morning than to get home.

"So I'm usually home by nine. Chris is asleep by then. I have something to eat, talk with Michael for a while, try to relax, and I usually am in bed by eleven, and am up again at six to do it all over again."

Jane does have some weekends off, but she often works one weekend day, or sometimes a portion of both. As every true professional knows, one doesn't become successful by counting on free weekends, unless one is counting on giving them up whenever duty calls.

In other words, Jane spends an average of eleven hours a day at the office. Her total commute takes about an hour, so that makes twelve hours devoted to her job. Subtract the twelve from twenty-four and that leaves twelve. Subtract the seven hours of sleep she usually gets, and Jane is left with five hours in a day, roughly, to call her own. And even that isn't accurate, because much of her morning time is used in preparation for work.

"I'm exhausted all the time," she says. "Right now, I'm the only person in my office who could be called a juggler or Superwoman, and most of the people I work with don't know how I do it. I don't know how I do it, either, but I don't have a choice about it. Much of my life seems to go by in a blur. I have no time for my friends, and no time for my favorite pastime, which is reading. I miss reading more than I can tell you. Until Chris was born I spent most of my free time with books. Now, if I manage to read a book at all, one novel can take six weeks.

"But the most difficult thing of all is Christopher. I try to devote weekends to him, going places and doing things and reading with him and just being with him. But sometimes I just have to be alone, and I yell at him to let me be for a while, and feel so guilty when I do I can't stand it. I feel guilty because I think we rushed him and forced him to grow up too quickly, and even though he loves his day-care center and his teachers and friends, he has spent ten hours a day away from his home and his parents since he was one year old. I had no choice, but I think that's too young. If he doesn't suffer from it—and there's no way for me to tell yet—he seems fine, I suffer from it. Michael isn't comfortable with it, either.

"We would like to have another baby and we have to decide soon, because I'm almost thirty-six. But we don't want to raise a second child on the run, the way we've raised Chris. But neither one of us can afford not to work full time, and neither one of us is ever going to make much more money than we make right now. Our fields are like that, they just don't pay very well, even when you get close to the top like I am.

"I have no idea what we're going to do, but I don't think I can go through another pregnancy and infancy and toddlerhood like Chris's. I'm spread so thin right now, I don't think there's anything left of me to devote to anything else. I'm an overworked professional, an overtired mother, a fair-weather friend, and a part-time wife. Superwoman, huh? Stuporwoman is more like it."

"Superwoman is not a fantasy woman, and not a creation of Madison Avenue, but she has a very, very difficult life task," says my consulting analyst. "There are many women today who simply cannot handle that many roles.

"It is upsetting to them to hear society say that Super-woman is something that's pretty easy to handle, all you need are proper management skills. And now our society seems to say that all women play this triple role just fine. But the implication that a good or worthwhile woman can and should handle so much is unfair and unrealistic.

"On the other hand, remember that the Superwoman can effectively counter a woman's fear of the old prohibitions against women being something more than a mother and housewife. That's a very good thing. And Superwoman can also counter unnecessary fears that it is impossible to be a professional, a wife and a mother. It is not impossible, nor should it be, so that's a good thing, too.

"But what I find interesting about this trend is that it has changed, or redefined, who the traditional enemy of the working woman is. Thirty or forty years ago a successful professional who wanted to have a child and to keep working faced a conflict between herself and *society.* Women were supposed to choose between professionalism and motherhood. The enemy was *externalized.* It was a society that said *no.*

"Today society says yes, go ahead, and pretends there's little or no conflict in this variety of roles. It's not just officially okay to be Superwoman, it's the newest official demand. So any woman who is having a hard time doing it all feels as if she is fighting not society, but herself. All the conflict is *internalized* now.

"Sometimes I think that it might have been much easier for professional women thirty or forty years ago, because it is always easier to fight against an outsider and a recognizable enemy than it is to fight within yourself. The problem women face now is that they live in a world that says, hey, you may have a few problems working this out, but really, everything's just fine. The war's been won. So if you're having anything more than a few small troubles, well then, something is very wrong with you. It's your problem and your deficiency. The system works just fine."

At first I disagreed with her—how could anything have been better for women forty years ago? But when I mull over what she says, I begin to agree. In terms of access and initial opportunity things are indisputably much better for women today. There's no contest. But if you stop to examine what begins to happen once you pass through the training program and the initial first job, it may have been easier years ago.

Those women were real pioneers, and pioneers don't have an easy time of it, but they are a special group with an aura, almost separate and unequal in heroic terms.

People take time and trouble over them, secretly or not-so-secretly admire and respect them, and help them out in ways both big and small. And often, what outsiders can't understand they are able to forgive, by categorizing a person as "eccentric" or "unusual" or simply "one of a kind," with special needs or desires that can be accommodated precisely because eccentricity or uniqueness can be so appealing.

But what happens when the one unique woman turns into 2, or 3, or 10 or 20 percent of the graduating class? What happens when people are unable to excuse, forgive, or make allowances (with affection and condescension) for behavior that is suddenly so widespread?

What happens is Superwoman, the creation of a whole class of people who are only doing what they are *supposed* to be doing. A whole class of successful women upon whom rests a whole new set of standards as well as most, if not all, of the old.

I am not sure that having it all is the most appropriate way to describe this state.

Nor do I think women properly reckoned the price of success.

For some women, though, no price is too high for success, and that is as it should be. A commonplace assumption is that earning extremely high salaries will make being Superwoman a simple and painless task, because money can buy the best day care and night care, maids, cooks, laundresses, perhaps even Jeeves himself. And there are women who earn this kind of income for whom Superwoman must be a joy.

And so I am ushered into an office in one of the foremost investment houses in the country, to interview a woman who is a graduate of the Harvard Business School, a firm vice-president, with an income well into six figures. I am interested in knowing, first of all, if she was frightened of the professional consequences of becoming a mother, and if so, what did she do to combat those fears?

"Scared? No, I was terrified," Julie says. "There were only a couple of women here before me who had children. One was fired and I really don't know why. The other one quit her job for a while to stay home with her baby, but now she's back. She's a vice-president, too, but she earns about one-half what I earn. She doesn't have a master's degree in business.

"But that's not the only reason she earns less. She also created a perception of herself here as a *mother*. She comes in at nine-fifteen and leaves every day at five to pick her child up. She let this corporation know right from the start that she had other requirements and personal needs that were unrelated to the corporation. You can't get away with that here.

"There was no way I was *not* going to have a baby just because of a job. You can't let people make those kinds of unwritten rules or legislate morality that way. But I have paid a price for having my daughter. I won't make as much money this year, and I get passed over for new accounts that require travel. And I'm also paying a price in terms of their perceptions of me.

"Before my daughter was born, I think they forgot I was a woman. There's no better way to remind them

173

than to work into your ninth month. Now I am not the same person in their eyes, I'm like their *wives*. So I'm very careful about how I behave at work. I never call home during the day to talk to my daughter or see how she is. If her baby-sitter needs me, if something is wrong, she'll call me. I never talk about her here, or discuss anything about children. At work I work, and I'm hoping they'll forget all about my child in a few years."

As Jane did, she runs through a typical day for me. The contrast is marked. Julie has a baby-sitter who arrives at eight A.M. and leaves at seven every evening, five days a week. She has a mother's helper who arrives at noon on Saturday and stays till "whenever." She and her husband also have other baby-sitters readily available for weeknights after her daily help leaves. She and her husband generally walk to work together, with no stops at a day-care center, and no rushing from the office to pick their daughter up before the center closes.

She tells me she sees her daughter about three hours a day, and that seems sufficient for the child, who is happy and doing fine with the baby-sitter. But in this case, I am less concerned with the effects of this arrangement on the child than I am with its effects on the mother; effects that become apparent when she tells me a story as I'm preparing to leave.

"I do my best to cater to their perceptions of what a professional woman should be, but there was one time when I wouldn't, and it was just a few weeks go. It was my daughter's first birthday and I decided to give her a party on that day in the afternoon. I came into work in the morning, but I left the office at twelve-thirty to go home for the party." She pauses and gives me a smile, a wide, triumphant smile. "When I left the office, I made sure *everyone* knew where I was going, and *why.*"

It doesn't sound like much, but that's its significance. For her this was an act of courage, daring, perhaps even rebellion, as well as a statement of who she is.

What she practices on a daily basis is more than simple juggling or apportioning eight hours for work, four for recreation, ninety minutes garnered for time to herself. She practices a form of repression and denial every day, to protect herself, and to conform and to succeed. The people she works for believe that professionalism and motherhood are mutually exclusive things. So she does what she must to downplay one identity so it will not harm the other.

But even she had to express what she felt at least once. Her money eases some of the pressures and does make life easier than life is for Jane.

Strip away the material differences, though, and they are sisters. The differences are in degree, not in kind.

"I'm reminded of the European upper classes of the past century," says my consulting therapist in response to Julie's story. "Those women gave birth and then literally gave up mothering. They turned their children over to wet nurses and nannies. From there, the children went to boarding schools and finishing schools, or college if they were male. When they were living at home, they were brought in for an hour a night to visit with Mummy and Daddy. In those days, women did this to free themselves to pursue a social life. Now women are doing it to free themselves for work and a professional life. An interesting development, isn't it?

"What this woman you've described to me is doing, in effect, is giving up mothering. She wouldn't see it that way, and probably wouldn't admit to it if she did. But with a baby-sitter all those hours five days a week, and an au pair girl on weekends, that's exactly what she's doing. Even when she is physically absent from the office and physically present at home there is rarely, if ever, a time when she alone is responsible for the care of her daughter.

"You see, the ultimate problem she faces at work is that all people have a general gut-level response toward *all* females. All women are always perceived partly as Mother, or mother figures. This can be a real problem for *childless* professional women. A professional woman who is in fact a mother is dealing with a double problem: the general response to all women plus the specific response to her because she has a child.

"In order to keep working successfully, she must deny the mother side of her as much as she possibly can. How much she does, and how well she does it, depends on the woman herself and the kind of work she does and maybe most importantly, the kind of atmosphere she works in.

"This woman works in a very negative atmosphere for a woman and a mother. In order to survive she denies motherhood not just at the office, but at home too. It's much easier for women to function when they have to deny motherhood only at the office, publicly, but not deny it at home. In either case it's a tough situation. In

176

the best of circumstances it makes a woman feel very split, and it can cause reactions such as constant fatigue and severe emotional stress. Women fare much better when they work in places where they can experience both sides of themselves at once, at least to some degree, without fear of reprisal. That way they can live a life that is integrated and enriched, not depleted and divided."

But the world of the corporate male turns on the principle of separation of the man from wife, family, and home, and on the idea that the best way to garner the energies and talent of employees is to make it clear that the best of one's time, energies, and loyalties belong to the company. When a woman enters that world, and agrees to abide by its code of honor, she is taking on a burden of immense proportions, and a conflict between her professional and personal self that may be irreconcilable for many.

This is, perhaps, the highest price of Superwoman's success.

"Having it all as a goal is just a little bit misguided, because it's a terrible oversimplification," says Ellen, as she hands her two-year-old son yogurt and a spoon. "No one can have it all. Try, and if you're very lucky, you might manage eighty percent. And the real question is, who gets short shrift in that equation? Someone is going to, depending on how you work things out. It might be you, your husband, or your child, but someone is going to lose out."

She is a former documentary news producer, who left

her business to give birth to her son, and chose to make a full-time career out of motherhood, at least for a few years.

"So many women are just fixated and obsessed with making it in the male corporate world that they feel utterly powerless and worthless if they don't compete and succeed in the corporation. They do not count the ability to carry a child and to give birth as a vital kind of power, and one that men are very jealous of. Nor do they consider caring for, educating, and playing with a child legitimate pursuits. I don't believe that being a mother, a nonworking mother, has to be a position of powerlessness and victimization and unimportance.

"If it becomes that, then I think that women are at fault in some way, although men are responsible for it too. It means that, once again, women have allowed themselves to be told who they are and who they must be. That's not liberation, if women believe they are something less if they want to be mothers and homemakers instead of lawyers or doctors. Someone else is still defining and dictating and women are still responding too passively.

"The tensions and pressures of my former job were just too great for me to consider working and having my son at the same time. Financially it's not necessary for me to work, but it would make things easier for us if I did. We don't live as well as we used to, and after ten years of earning my own money I'm sometimes uncomfortable not earning any.

"But I knew my child would be a hindrance to my

178

career and a source of constant professional conflict, and so I made a choice. Now that he's two, I'm starting to look at the job market again, but I'm not sure that's it's time to return yet, or even if I want to.

"I suppose that if someone asked me if I have it all, I'd say yes, but I'd mean it differently than they do. I'm thirty-two years old and I've been a single professional and a married one, I have a solid record of good employment in a prestigious field, and I'm also a mother and homemaker, something else I've always wanted to do. All these different things have contributed to making me who I am. It's not necessary that I do them all at the same time as proof of my competence or my worth. If doing everything at once is having it all, my response is, *you* can have *it*."

"I refuse to be all things to all people, and I refuse to wear myself down to a nub doing so many things at one time," says Andrea indignantly. "My mother calls those women the new slave class and she snorts at them. They trade one form of slavery in the house for a new form that includes most or all of the duties of the housewife, plus much more. It's twice as demanding and stress-filled. How can anybody look at that so-called ideal and want to be that? Those women must be so exhausted all the time. I don't know how they do it, or why they'd even want to."

"I don't understand those women, I don't understand how they can live," Sarah says, echoing Andrea. "How can they rest? Where is some peace and quiet for them?

179

Everyone needs time to themselves. I watch those women and I pity them. I would never want to be like that."

Andrea and Sarah react to Superwoman by assuming that they will be lucky enough to have a measure of choice regarding career and motherhood, that financial imperatives to work full time at their current pace will not exist. They may be right, and they may be lucky, because they will be free to experiment and discover what route is best for them, and for their children.

But their visceral reaction to Superwoman is based largely on their knowledge of what it costs in terms of emotional and mental energy to be successful in their profession. They know from experience how stressful work can be, and how much of themselves they have left over for commitments to other people and things.

It's almost as if our society has developed a new double standard for men and women, this time based on stress instead of sexual mores. Stress is a popular topic, good for sociological studies and three-part, in-depth analyses in newspapers, eye-catching for a *Time* or *Newsweek* cover story. Almost without exception, experts conclude what is already self-evident: we live in a world and a society with almost intolerable and insurmountable stress and pressure levels. If the threat of nuclear war or international terrorism doesn't get you down, crime in the streets, skyrocketing drug and alcohol abuse, the cost of living, noise pollution, air pollution, filth, crowding, gridlock, or paying your taxes will.

The fabric of daily life today can be enough to drive the staunchest and strongest running for cover or escape. Stress makes people sick, either physically or mentally or both. Stress is considered a national problem, an epidemic of sorts, and all sorts of methods of coping with it, from transcendental meditation, to diet, to exercise, to clinics that specialize in stress therapy, have sprung up, almost like little sideline industries. And the stress the experts talk about, the factors that create it, affect everyone, men, women, and children. It knows no barriers of race or class or religion.

But the eighties woman takes all this in stride, and more. She takes on all the stress of daily life and positively revels in it, so much so that she adds even more demanding tasks and chores and roles, and she rarely turns a hair. She is a full-time working professional, a wife, a mother. She does her work, keeps her marriage alive, gives quality time or more to her children, and runs a house too, with or without domestic help. And comes home at night to give an intimate little dinner party for twenty of her most cherished friends.

Men seem quick to discuss the trials of their work, their stresses and pressures, how demanding their jobs are, and how much they need and appreciate sympathy and empathy, care, and even coddling from the women in their lives. They need peace and quiet so often when they return after their grueling day at the office. But not so for women. Now one's ambition is supposed to be performing in an office all day, performing at home, in fact, performing around the clock.

If this isn't a double standard, I don't know what could possibly qualify for the term.

And so sometimes I wonder, really wonder, how any of us can, with a straight face, call this an ideal, or a liberation, or a major improvement in women's status.

The rat race is over. The rats won.

9

The High Cost of Liberation

I am at a playground in Connecticut with my five-year-old nephew and his little friend. They have raced madly from the jungle gym and merry-go-round to the swings and then the seesaw. I stand nearby, watching, keeping a wary eye out lest someone start to tumble off. I watch them go up and down, up and down, first high, then low, on top and then on the bottom. Their rhythm hypnotic. It mesmerizes me. My vision clouds, then clears, and I see myself, not them, on both sides of the seesaw. I take my ride, straddling both ends of the board, perhaps playing both ends against the middle, searching for a balance. The seesaw seems a perfect symbol for female life.

When someone sees only one side of a question, he or she probably has an easier time of it. A kind of righteousness pervades daily life and propels you through its conflicts, reducing the complexities and vagaries of existence into a kind of formula, whatever the formula may be. The formula dictates much of your behavior: opinions, actions, reactions, and responses. Those on your side wear white hats. Everyone else is clad in black.

I am sometimes extremely uncomfortable with the knowledge that I no longer see one side of the question but see both sides all too clearly.

I can construct, quite honestly, an argument in favor of one viewpoint, and then turn right around and make an equally good case for the opposing viewpoint, without pausing for breath.

184

The ups and downs of success are, on the most obvious level, the times you love your work and the times you cannot stand it. The times you are certain that you were right to invest so much of yourself in a career, at the possible expense of a personal life, and the days when you believe nothing could be less important, or constricting, than success.

But the ups and downs go deeper than this. The seesawing comes from being able to see, all too clearly, both sides of the question. Being able to make a good case for feminism—for career, for independence, for success, for economic control over your life, for mothers working by choice, for day care—and an equally good case *not* for antifeminism, but for living life as a more "traditional" female. Wavering between what seem to be the undeniable truths of the women's movement that have helped to change your life permanently and the longing for a less rigid, more flexible and tolerant interpretation of those truths.

In fact, the highest cost of liberation may be the constant feeling of forever being torn, of being pulled unceasingly in opposite directions. Wishing one day for success and the next for marriage or children or both; living in fear that to give up work for some period of time to take care of a baby means losing all one's self-esteem and separate identity; feeling guilty and torn because one has not given up work to stay home and care for an infant; and wondering why, if women are supposed to be in a position of almost unlimited choice, even to the extent of having it all if they so choose, their so-called choices don't really feel like much of a choice at all. It's a "damned if you do, damned if you don't" kind of situation, a Catch-22. Whatever position you settle on, whatever choices you make, a whole chorus of outsiders, social critics, social scientists, feminists, antifeminists, conservatives, liberals, and radicals will be waiting to comment. You're right. No, you're wrong. You're destroying the family. You're spoiling your child. Don't get a nurse, use day care. Don't trust your child to a stranger, stay at home.

Meanwhile, during this process of decision and choice, we encourage women to choose based largely on the assumption that it is possible to fully integrate the identities of professional, wife, and mother with little or no trouble, no high emotional and physical price tag; we imply, if not state outright, that these women are somehow better than the others; or else we assure single women that their work is everything, the only thing, that counts, while behind their backs raising cruel and unkind questions and comments about their sexuality, desirability, and lack of a man.

This assumption that there is no constant conflict between a successful professional life and a successful personal one for women is in part directly traceable to the long-standing insistence of the women's movement that women are really no "different" from men, given the education and opportunity to work and to achieve in the same arenas in which men achieve; and that any differences in female behavior exist because they are sociologically induced and the result of male-dominated social conditioning. There is probably no doubt that, up to a point, this analysis is correct. I believe it. I accept it. I have seen plenty of evidence of it. But now I cannot quite believe it to the degree I once did. I do not accept it as the complete truth, the sole answer, for there is other evidence to the contrary. But it was (and perhaps too often still is) easier to push aside the whole question of sociology versus biology, and insist that biology plays little or no part in the equation—even though questions of biology were, and still are, ill researched and unresolved, a question mark for all of us.

Only now are women psychologists, ones like Carol Gilligan at Harvard, really starting to explore the female psyche, and once again the questions of sex differences arise and along with them, the idea that women may have concerns that are *different,* but *just as valid* as men's.

The new work begins with the premise—still controversial—that women tend to mother, or nurture. Because of this, they have a different viewpoint toward life than men. They make consistent moral judgments that men feel are deficient. Their moral outlook on life causes them to make sacrifices in a way that men have traditionally labeled "masochistic." And women have a tendency to feel stress in the lives of people they love as if it were their very own.

In short, before now, women's psychological development was measured against men's and the male ideal, and so women were always found to be lacking in some way when compared with the "superior" male. What the new women's psychology does is to formulate a new and different definition of maturity—one in which women simply have different priorities regarding human experience than men have.

This is no small thing, especially now, as the conflicts between work and motherhood, the professional and the personal, become more and more apparent.

And so, while women have pursued success, and having it all, for their own personal satisfaction and gain, they have also been willing to swallow a very male definition of what success is, what worthy pursuits are, and what inspires admiration and respect. Perhaps the new women's psychology will help women to feel more comfortable with themselves in the coming years, if they do not feel that "having it all" or success on men's terms is necessarily the best way to live. I am not really sure that it is possible for most of us to fuse the personal and professional into one smooth, charming, comfortable, and competent whole—doing everything our mothers did, and everything our fathers did as well.

Perhaps the saddest thing about the past twenty years' worth of feminist thought is that it helped to smash much of the, old order—and in many ways deservedly so—but has been seemingly incapable of creating a new order and a structure for living that would incorporate real options and, consequently, true equality. It is not enough—it was never enough—to merely discard the fifties middle class suburban housewife for the Superwoman of the seventies and eighties. There is something architecturally unsound about this design for living passed from one generation to the next.

Sometimes I feel as if I've been left standing around,

holding the biological bag, so to speak, along with diplomas, Phi Beta Kappa keys, doctorates, and the uncomfortable knowledge that I can never construct a sound dwelling with these tools alone.

The problem, of course, is how to proceed when one has had one's eyes opened, one's self "enlightened." When one has been reeducated to understand the long and brutal history of women, so often one of terror, degradation, blame, punishment, and exclusion. When one acknowledges a legacy in which theology, philosophy, psychology, law, even language and custom, conspire to disgrace, debase, shame, or ignore us. And to assure us of our constant inferiority to the male of the species.

Here come the gibberings and the I dunnos; search me; your guess is as good as mine. How-tos are not my forte. I mistrust them. I am trying to school myself into accepting ambivalence as the fundamental human condition, and yet I may be asked to reject ambivalence and assume that ten-point programs and manifestoes can be fashioned for general consumption.

No, they can't. But women do have some insights to offer, some ideas, however utopian, about the ways in which women change the level of the debate, revamp earlier solutions, and look for new ways to perceive themselves and their roles.

Some women began with very simple things: the way women dress for work. A clear antipathy toward outward manifestations of maleness seems to be developing.

"Forget those dress-for-success books that encourage

women to wear suits and ties and to avoid soft dresses," says Andrea, a lawyer. "If I see one more of those books I think I'll be sick. They're ridiculous. How insulting to all of us that someone thinks we're so stupid or sheltered that we can't figure out for ourselves what is appropriate for work and what isn't. The best thing everyone can do is to find her own style and develop it. If that means wearing dresses with some frivolous trimming because you think you look better and feel more comfortable in them, wear them.

"Nothing disguises the fact that you're a woman and nothing changes the fact that men are sometimes uncomfortable with your femininity and your presence. Just be who you are and the chances are that people will feel more comfortable with you—and that works to your professional advantage."

Another common theme: women must face some very hard choices that men do not face, and they must accept this fact rather than quarrel with it.

"I was talking with a woman last week who was *carrying on* about how unfair it is that women have to worry about maternity leave and child care and dropping out of the work force for a while, when men don't really have to worry about any of it at all. She kept repeating, 'It isn't *fair,* why do *I* have to worry when men don't, it just isn't *fair.*' She was really whining," says Jane, the magazine editor.

"Well, she's right in some ways, but in other ways she's wrong. She's missing the point. Part of the process of growing up and becoming an adult is learning to accept some of life's limitations gracefully. That's called *maturity.* Acccepting somewhat less than whatever you dreamed about having is almost everyone's lot in life.

"For me, the past five or six years of my life have been a lesson in learning to accept some of the limitations life's thrown at me, and some of those limitations seem to be part of being female. Part of the fact that as a woman I made choices about my work and my personal life and having a child that were much more significant choices to me than to my husband. They affect his life, but not as radically as they have affected mine.

"I do not think that is unfair. It's pointless for me to sit around, day and night, whining and resentful and angry because my husband hasn't made the same kind of trade-offs I have. I don't believe he is responsible for that.

"What is *unfair* is that my son's day care costs seven thousand dollars a year. It's even more unfair that we get almost no tax break for the cost of the day care. It's unfair that my company doesn't provide low-cost day care for its employees. Those are wrongs, and they can be righted over time.

"But this breast-beating, foot-stamping, petulant stuff about the unfairness of being female because it involves some hard decisions about work and children and personal life is a useless, pointless waste of energy. It's a turn-off, too. The right to have everything made easy for you, so that you can earn a six-figure income, get married, have kids, live the good life, never worry about money or child care—this having-it-all stuff—is not a God-given or constitutional right. There are limitations everywhere. Men have limitations, but you'd never

191

know it to hear this woman talk. All of them earn huge salaries, run corporations, and never worry about anything at all, ever.

"Like too many other women, she thinks that the most important thing you can achieve in life is a high salary and an impressive-sounding job. She's helped to contribute to the demeaning of legitimate work as a nurse or teacher or secretary. Those are fine ways for women to earn a living, and even though they don't pay as much as they should, those women are compensated by having regular hours, free weekends, and more control over their time and their personal lives. Secretaries and teachers anyway.

"There is much to be said for choosing those careers if you want to have children, be able to spend more time with them, and be more involved with your family and your home. It's a trade-off, and one most men just don't feel they have to make. Women are more apt to make this trade-off because of their ties to their children. I don't think that's a terrible thing. Besides, you can really get tired of hearing people say that women have to set their sights really high professionally, as if anything else is worthless, and as if every man in the world is a high-powered executive knocking down a huge salary. Face it, most of them are not.

"When I get tired of working full time and rarely seeing my husband and my son, I tell my friends I would give anything, just anything, to quit being successful. They don't believe me. They tell me I'd be bored in a week, staying at home and taking care of Christopher, and running the house.

192

"They're wrong. I know what I'd do, and I'd enjoy every minute of it. I'd get pregnant and have the second child I want and I would finally have time to get to know my son.

"I would love to be able to take a few years off, away from work, but when I say that to other women, they immediately respond by telling me I'd never be able to get another job as an editor at the high level where I am now. Leaving a career for a period of time means ruining the career. It may be true at the moment, but nothing makes me angrier than listening to other women say this like it's written in stone. Why do women do this?

"If anything, women should be challenging those statements, and trying to get men to see that a year's absence from a career, or even more, should not mean that women are unfit to return to their job at the level they left it. I've been working in magazines for fifteen years or more. Could anyone possibly think that I would forget, or be incompetent, because I stopped doing it for twelve or eighteen months?

"But the way things are now, women are punished for wanting to have a child and to continue working, unless they do it exactly the way their company wants them to. And women themselves haven't done anything at all about it. They just take the male line, too, and rush to assure them that once maternity leave is over, everything will be exactly like before, and they'll never, ever know there's a baby somewhere.

"As far as I'm concerned, that's not such a major breakthrough. Women have been doing that for decades. In fact, my mother did it. We had to lie about my little brother and pretend he didn't exist, because my mother wasn't permitted to have more than three children, and she had four. As far as I can see, what's different now is just the numbers of women who work, not the way people regard them, or the way companies treat them once they have children.

"I would like to see the whole tack of the women's movement change, from the 'Yes, we're no different from the guys' attitude to 'We *are* different, and just as important, and we'd better change the system to accommodate us.' Women are more than fifty percent of the population, so it's time to end the tyranny of the male minority."

Jane is echoed by Jamie, a former insurance broker from Milwaukee, who left work after more than a decade to have two children.

"Right now what we value is work and success as the business world defines them, and that pretty much excludes valuing motherhood and the home. I think that women should start to fight to create a new, postindustrial view of women and motherhood and work.

"At one time women at home were given respect and were seen as performing valuable work. That view started to diminish as society became more industrialized, and men went off to work and left women at home. The same technology that made men's work possible also reduced some of the hard, physical labor women did in the home. Washers and dryers and vacuums and dishwashers made things much easier and women at home had more free time. I guess by the fifties that attitude became sort of institutionalized: the lazy housewife, the spoiled, lazy housewife, who had nothing to do all day but play with a few appliances and take care of kids. To me, that's like saying men with white-collar jobs don't know the real meaning of work because they don't break their backs every day doing construction.

"What women have to do is reeducate men, and themselves in some cases, to try and see motherhood as a legitimate and purposeful *phase* of a woman *and man's* life *together.* If motherhood can be seen to be a phase of an entire life, a part of the identity rather than the entire one, then maybe devoting oneself to motherhood for a period of time can be respected again. To insist that it is valuable only when a woman is working full time too is absurd.

"I got pregnant by accident, and I decided that if I made the choice to have my child, I had to also choose to be a mother for some portion of my life. After more than nine years of doing a damn good job in the insurance business, I have to believe there's room for me again if I want to return. I look at these years taking care of my two children as a sabbatical, and I'm determined to make other people see things my way."

Utopian, head in the clouds, they don't understand the way things work: profit and loss, how to *run a business.* The entire fabric of corporate American life would no doubt collapse if women were permitted the freedom to take a leave of absence, and have someone else fill in for them.

Somehow I find that a little hard to swallow, even though I am supposed to nod wisely, if regretfully, and agree. This collapse of American business that would no doubt occur if we were to institutionalize leaves of absence for working mothers presumes that all women employed by a company want to have children; that they will all be giving birth and be absent at exactly the same time; and that all of them would choose to exercise a leave option, when some would no doubt be back at work in six weeks.

The real problem with Jane and Jamie's ideas is not with the *mechanics* of their solution. If every corporation in America woke up tomorrow determined to implement their views, they could do so. They have done far more difficult things.

The problem is the prejudice against it—automatic, knee-jerk, perhaps unconscious even. But motherhood is our last bastion of the worst kind of bias and bigotry. It remains the tool by which women can be ultimately, and "legitimately," excluded from the world of men in business. It's the means used to force women to make a "choice" that is not much of a choice at all.

"Do it our way, the way it's been done, the men's way, the only way." So that is exactly what women have done, grateful for the opportunity, and frightened to challenge the conventional wisdom. To do anything else is to invite the remarks: "I knew we shouldn't hire a woman—they just want to have children." "They're a bad risk, a bad investment, and they don't want it badly enough, anyway. They just quit and have kids."

And this will continue, legitimized and institutionalized, unless women choose to do something about it.

Like the study quoted by *Fortune* that concluded that

the presence of women in large numbers in an office did not reduce discrimination but increased it, it is not enough to say that things will change in time when enough women become managers. Not only are women not becoming managers in great numbers, but women themselves can be the worst offenders. One of the saddest stories I heard was told by a woman from Tennessee, a banker, whose division at the office was run by another woman. She believed, naively, that her boss would sympathize with her request for extra leave without pay, so that she could stay home with her baby for six months. "Under no circumstances," said her boss. "There will be no special privileges here for women. You come back when your maternity leave is up or you don't come back at all." This woman told me that once her anger passed, she understood her boss, although she didn't agree with her. Threatened, insecure in her own position, determined to prove that management had not made a mistake by giving her her job, she outmaled men at their own game. And so the banker went back to work. She had no choice.

Her story is commonplace. It makes all this talk of choice and change and . . . liberation . . . sound awfully hollow.

Success has not been nearly so . . . successful as we hoped.

It's hard to take pleasure or satisfaction in the latest recitation of statistics about women working or women attending graduate school. They are a misleading measurement in too many ways. Especially as an indicator of the quality of life for women.

197

Single or married, mothers or professionals or both, most of us still straddle our seesaws, teeter-tottering forever between a history we have tried to disown and a present that offers no real replacement for a rejected past.

I drive my friend, my oldest friend, the one on whom I have relied for so long, and her one-year-old daughter to John F. Kennedy International Airport. I am putting them on a flight to Paris, where they will join my friend's husband. His corporation has moved him to Paris for three years.

She is not leaving a job behind. She quit her job as a graphic designer when she was eight months' pregnant. Instead, she does free-lance design work when she can. But she is leaving behind a whole way of life, everything that is familiar and comfortable now shipped, or stored, or rented to another family for three years.

She is frightened. She knows no one in Paris and does not speak the language. While her husband works, with a ready-made circle of colleagues and days filled with purpose, she will be forced to start from scratch, to find friends and build a new life not just for her, but for her daughter too.

Fifteen years ago, or twenty, she would have been considered lucky. Fortunate to be married to someone whose career gave her the chance to live in a place like Paris.

But she sees it with a jaundiced eye now. She sees herself as a mother and housewife "following" her husband abroad because of his work. Sacrificing her own,

THE HIGH COST OF LIBERATION

and a victim, a captive, of someone else's life at the expense of her own.

We stand by the gate, waiting for the flight to be called, and to me she looks no different from the seventeen-year-old who asked me to help her carry a lamp up three flights of stairs to her room next to mine in our dorm. She was beautiful then as she is now, tall and slim in a pale blue linen blazer the color of her eyes, her blond hair a cap curling around her face, her daughter a tiny image of her, cradled in her arms.

There is nothing left to say now, but when they call her flight, I turn and speak.

"Don't worry, it'll be okay," I say lamely.

She looks at me for a moment, and I am afraid she is going to cry. But she does not.

"Yeah, it will have to be," she says. "But I want to tell you something before I go, okay? Scared as I am, I can't wait to get away from here, Hilary. That's what I feel most of all, not fear or excitement, just relief at escaping.

"I can't wait to get away from people asking me what I *do*—and when I say I take care of my daughter, they look at me like I'm crazy, or something less than human. At parties and at dinners they turn away and look for someone else to talk to. I'm so tired of dragging out my credentials as a graphic designer and explaining what I used to do so that people will pay attention to me—you know what I mean?"

I nod. I do.

"Ever since Erica was born I've felt this way, apologetic and defensive about myself and, and—well, deficient. I can't stand it much longer. I don't know how to fight it, anymore, either. It's got to—it will be better in Paris, won't it?"

"Yes, of course, sure it will," I babble. "Much better, you'll see."

Her smile thanks me. We hug goodbye. Erica wails. Then she turns and walks away, loaded down with daughter and a carry-on bag full of things for her, looking much the same as I once pictured myself, struggling off to another assignment at yet another stadium, in yet another city.

She disappears down the jetway and I head back toward the car, disturbed by her words. As I drive along the Van Wyck to the Grand Central Parkway, across the Triboro and down the FDR Drive, her words vibrate in my head, a sad refrain, and they take on a life of their own.

I hope that Paris will be better for her. That whatever form the women's movement has taken there, it will be kinder and more tolerant, more supportive and less cruel, than the one we have fashioned for ourselves here.

And what I hope for even more, I think as I maneuver the car into a parking place for the night, is that it will be better for her, and for all of us, when the day arrives for her homecoming.

ACKNOWLEDGMENTS

There are many people who made this book possible and who deserve recognition and thanks. First, my agent and long-time family friend Bill Adler, whose support, encouragement and belief in this project were invaluable. Thanks, too, to my editor Joan Sanger for her enthusiasm and her help. Janice Kaplan's advice, criticisms and suggestions were also invaluable, as was her ability to tolerate me when writing made me intolerable. Chris DeNovellis helped immensely with the research. My husband Patrick not only read every page of every draft and gently offered advice and criticism, but also encouraged the sometimes difficult transition from producer to writer. Finally, special thanks to the women I interviewed. They trusted a total stranger with very private and personal information on very sensitive topics. Without them and their candor, there would be no book.

201

ABOUT THE AUTHOR

Hilary Cosell attended Sarah Lawrence College and graduated magna cum laude from New York University. She received a master's degree in journalism from Northwestern University. For five years she wrote and produced the SportsJournal segment of NBC's "SportsWorld" and was nominated four times for an Emmy. She lives in New York City with her husband. This is her first book.